Explore! Glacier National Park and Montana's Flathead Valley

Help Us Keep This Guide Up to Date

Every effort has been made by the authors and editors to make this guide as accurate and useful as possible. However, many things can change after a guide is published—trails are rerouted, regulations change, techniques evolve, facilities come under new management, etc.

We would love to hear from you concerning your experiences with this guide and how you feel it could be improved and kept up to date. While we may not be able to respond to all comments and suggestions, we'll take them to heart and we'll also make certain to share them with the authors. Please send your comments and suggestions to the following address:

The Globe Pequot Press
Reader Response/Editorial Department
P.O. Box 480
Guilford, CT 06437

Or you may e-mail us at:

editorial@GlobePequot.com

Thanks for your input, and happy trails!

Exploring Series

Explore! Glacier National Park and Montana's Flathead Valley

Jane and Bert Gildart

FALCONGUIDES ®

GUILFORD, CONNECTICUT
HELENA, MONTANA
AN IMPRINT OF THE GLOBE PEQUOT PRESS

FALCONGUIDES®

Copyright © 2007 Morris Book Publishing, LLC

Maps by Mapping Specialists © Morris Book Publishing, LLC
Photos by Bert and Jane Gildart, unless otherwise credited.

Library of Congress Cataloging-in-Publication Data

Gildart, Jane.
    A Falconguide to Glacier National Park and Montana's Flathead Valley / Jane and Bert Gildart.
        p. cm. — (A Falcon guide) (Exploring series)
    Includes index.
    ISBN 978-0-7627-3644-7
    1. Hiking—Montana—Glacier National Park—Guidebooks. 2. Trails—Montana—Glacier National Park—Guidebooks. 3. Glacier National Park (Mont.)—Guidebooks. 4. Flathead River Valley (B.C. and Mont.)—Guidebooks. I. Gildart, Robert C. II. Title. III. Series. IV. Series: Exploring series

GV199.42.M92G5642 2007
796.5109786'52—dc22   2006015907

Manufactured in the United States of America
First Edition/Third Printing

For Angie (Gildart) and her husband Will Friedner,
but particularly for the indomitable Halle Mae.
She's four at this writing and already quite the trouper.

Sacred Dancing Cascade and McDonald Creek are set against a backdrop of snow-covered mountains, including Mount Brown.

Contents

Acknowledgments

As always, no book is ever without the help, advice, and friendship of many. That is certainly true in this case. It was gratifying that, from everyone we talked with, we received enthusiasm for this book. Such is the devotion that Montanans have for these wonderful places, Glacier National Park and the Flathead Valley.

Carol and Bill Edgar and Elaine Snyder gave freely of their time, expertise, and suggestions. Dori Hamilton, executive director of the Flathead Convention and Visitor Bureau, provided "hard to find" information. Many thanks to readers Sue McDonald of Montana Fish, Wildlife and Parks, and Melissa Wilson, public affairs specialist at Glacier National Park. Thanks also to "Hutch" Hutchison for suggesting ski trails in the park. Jerry Sawyer, Flathead Lake manager, was a great help with the Flathead Lake Marine Trail. Bill Schneider, acquisitions editor for the Globe Pequot Press gave (as usual) tremendous help, as did Russ Schneider.

And kudos once again to Globe Pequot associate editor Julie Marsh, an intrepid and valued editor.

McDonald Creek in winter, just below Sacred Dancing Cascade, can be accessed from Lake McDonald Trailhead.

Introduction

Some 230 years ago, when the mountain range containing Glacier National Park was first seen by Europeans, adventurers were prompted to call this the Land of Shining Mountains. Yet another applicable catch phrase could be Land of Glorious Adversity, for contemporary scientists tell us that violent forces created this inspiring land where mountains reach up to touch the sky.

In part, because of these geological and geographical variations—implied, of course, by these catch names—Glacier is also a land of vast and incredible natural diversity. Five habitat types occur, which are largely determined by weather. Climate, in turn, is affected by the vagaries of altitude—which in Glacier is extreme. Here, relief varies from about 3,000 feet near Lake McDonald on the park's west side to more than 10,000 feet at Mount Cleveland on the park's east side. In between these extremes is a considerable variety of plant and animal species the eons have left as a part of their legacy, as a part of this Land of Shining Mountains, this Land of Glorious Adversity.

Catch-names tell a lot, and likewise Montana has its devotees who have ascribed a term that reflects their feelings. For many The Last Best Place is the expression that best describes not just Montana's Big Sky Country, but more specifically, the way most feel about this gorgeous area we call home, the Flathead Valley.

Located just south of Glacier, some 60 or so miles from the Canadian border, the Flathead (as it is commonly known) has become a mecca for visitors and explorers from all over the United States and foreign countries. The Rocky Mountains engulf us while the Flathead River flows past Kalispell, spilling into Flathead Lake, the largest body of freshwater west of the Mississippi River. Interestingly, two of the forks of the Flathead originate in or near Glacier National Park, while the other originates in the Bob Marshall Wilderness, another component of the Flathead. Together Glacier, the Bob Marshall, and the Great Bear Wilderness Area form a contiguous land mass

In the Jewel Basin Hiking Area mountain goats are often found sharing trails with hikers.

that has enabled scientists to introduce yet another descriptive name: the Northern Continental Divide Grizzly Bear ecosystem. Though the name is self-descriptive, Glacier is at the hub of a series of conduits that lead not only throughout these three areas, but into the heart of the Flathead Valley.

The valley is surrounded by more than a million acres of public lands that include national forest and several wilderness areas. Hiking, biking, fishing, photography, boating, skiing, golfing, snowmobile riding, hunting, hundreds of bird species, and wildlife galore all exist in this one area. Add to this delicious mix the fact that Glacier National Park, The Crown of the Continent, contributes ecological resources to the Flathead, and you can easily see why tourism remains the valley's main industry.

Several main arteries lead into the Flathead and Glacier region. From Missoula, U.S. Highway 93 threads northwest reaching the southern part of Flathead Valley in about an hour. Yet another hour will find you linking with U.S. Highway 2 leading into West Glacier, one entrance to Glacier National Park.

From the east, driving west, US 2 will take you past U.S. Highway 89 to Browning, which provides easy access to Glacier, or a continuation around the southern portion of Glacier National Park, again, to West Glacier. Several major airlines, such as Delta, Northwest, Big Sky, and Horizon Air, also serve the valley into Kalispell's Glacier International Airport.

Glacier and the entire valley abound with accommodations to suit the taste of everyone, from luxurious western lodges to state and private campgrounds. You'll never lack for restaurants either, for the Flathead offers a full range of choices, from fast-food standbys and casual dining spots to fine restaurants and microbrew pubs. We have not documented any restaurants or places of lodging in this book, but all information on eating and sleeping can be easily obtained by contacting the Flathead Convention and Visitor Bureau in Kalispell. See appendix A for contact information.

You'll find that each settlement, town, or city in the Flathead is unique and has something special to offer as well as some fascinating history to tell. Kalispell is the principal town and our main retail hub. Whitefish, which sits at the base of the Big Mountain Ski Resort, is more of a resort town. Columbia Falls is known as the Gateway to Glacier. In addition to these three main communities, you'll find the valley has many smaller settlements, such as Bigfork, Somers, Lakeside, Polson, and Yellow Bay, all located along Flathead Lake.

One of the best things about Glacier and the Flathead is that, no matter the season, there is always something fascinating to explore and to do. The weather is (usually) surprisingly mild for such a northern location. Summer temperatures often reach into the 90s, but the humidity is low. Fall is a favorite season for some residents, particularly if there's an Indian summer, which begins about mid-September.

January averages from 25 to 30 degrees, and while snow in some years can be awesome (in 1996 our neighbor literally skied off the roof of his house), it's unusual for snow in the valley to pile high or to linger long. That's not true, however, in Glacier, the northern part of the Flathead, where the plowing and opening of Logan Pass along the park's famed Going-to-the-Sun Road is an annual attraction.

Whatever the season and whatever your interests, we know you'll have unforgettable experiences in Glacier National Park and the Flathead Valley—by whatever name you choose to call them. We also are sure that you'll find the people of the valley, in fact, in all of Montana, to be special folks. Space requires that we not write of everything doable here, but rather, we offer a sampling and encourage you to explore further on your own.

Happy travels!

Alder Creek is located along Going-to-the-Sun Road in Glacier National Park.

Section I:
Glacier National Park

Mount Jackson supports one of the park's most significant glaciers, Jackson Glacier.

Chapter 1
Warming Up to Glacier

With a hushed whisper my wife Janie asked me to stop. "Listen," she said. "What do you hear?" The answer was nothing. Absolutely nothing.

Grandeur spread before us, and although its existence was the result of magnificent motion, nothing stirred. From my years of working in the land known as Glacier National Park, I knew the park was the result of motion that vacillated between calm and an overwhelming cacophony of sounds—a land born of fire, quenched by torrential rains, inundated by vast seas, forced upward by uneven surface deposits, and then gouged by continental ice sheets that came and went on at least four different occasions. Magnificent forces all—forces that require motion—but we stood quietly overwhelmed by the brooding silence.

Overhead, clouds drifted, propelled by some abstract force; nearby, banks of glacier lilies grew adjacent to remnants of tired glaciers. Here was the primordial—the essence of the wilderness—and I knew the country harbored creatures that could send the adrenaline surging. During one of the thirteen summers I'd worked in the park as a backcountry ranger, I'd been followed by a grizzly as the wind shrieked like so many banshees. Country that can evoke such memories even when it is silent should be examined and cherished. We stood in awe.

Designated a national park in 1910, Glacier was set aside because of its scenic splendor and because of its wildlife, which includes some 60 species of mammals, over 270 birds, and an estimated 1,300 plants. To trudge through this 1.1-million-acre park would take weeks. For the quickest overview drive Going-to-the-Sun Road. The late newsman and travel writer Charles Kuralt called it "one of America's most beautiful highways."

The alpine section of the 50-mile-long Going-to-the-Sun Road is open only during summer and early fall. Snow usually plugs the road's high-altitude passes nine months of the year. Even in early June, traffic may be slowed by snow-removal machines finishing their task of blasting out 50- to 70-foot-deep drifts.

From West Glacier to the summit of the road at Logan Pass, motorists gain almost 3,500 feet in altitude. About a quarter of the way up, the road plunges into a tunnel, its windows framing Heaven's Peak, one of the park's most spectacular mountains. Several hundred yards beyond, the road makes a switchback and appears like a shelf on the face of a perpendicular cliff.

Janie was not always comfortable with heights, and her calm surprised me. Off to our right, only a small retaining wall separated us from a 100-foot drop. On the other side loomed a sheer-faced cliff.

Going-to-the-Sun Road, built in the 1930s, takes you through an alpine setting that may be the country's most beautiful.

Going-to-the-Sun Road peaks at 6,646-foot-high Logan Pass. A visitor center provides interpretive literature while naturalists suggest ways to get to know and enjoy the area.

Trails from Logan Pass enter the park's interior. One trail leads to the Hidden Lake Overlook and a geological feature known as hanging gardens. The trail also provides sweeping views. To the north stretch the Livingston and Lewis Ranges, which hurtle across the Canadian border. To the southeast lies the patch of turquoise that is St. Mary Lake and an exit of the famed road from the park. Beyond that, the Great Plains roll to the horizon, forming the loose boundary with today's Blackfeet Indian Reservation.

By virtue of its name, the park implies the overwhelming presence of glaciers that once ground their way deeper into valleys. Ice sheets do exist in the park and one, Grinnell Glacier, can easily be reached from Many Glacier. Assembling our day packs, Janie and I boarded a cruise boat that took us to the upper end of Josephine Lake. As the boat progressed across the lake, a naturalist explained a bit about glaciers and mentioned that the park is more appropriately named for past glacial activity, which we would see at Grinnell.

Getting to Grinnell was part of the fun. As we hiked up a steep trail, we waded through bushes lush with berries. We picked a handful of ripe huckleberries, savoring for a moment their sweetness. A wind blew, and to prevent surprising a bear feeding from another berry patch, the naturalist suggested we sing.

At Grinnell the naturalist described the glacier, telling us it first had been measured in 1887, when it extended more than 480 feet. A warming trend over the past century had reduced the glacier to 255 feet. "The warming trend also eliminated or reduced many other glaciers," he said. "Today only about fifty glaciers remain. Some are less than twenty acres and are so obscure they are nameless." Still, he added, the park's features broadcast immense glacial activity such as glacial scratches, glacial polish, and the knife-shaped features called arêtes. Then he pointed out these features that stood quietly in this huge amphitheater, waiting for another audition.

Again the park was silent, but I knew it could be otherwise. Once in winter I drove to the valley's trailhead. Several hours later I skied across the ice-covered lake. The day was warm, melting the snow along the flanks and kicking off avalanches that rumbled down the slope. The park can be moody—and sometimes incredibly noisy.

Many Glacier Valley offers a variety of other activities. In spring, blue grouse stake out territories, defending them with ventriloquistic hooting. In fall, bighorn rams congregate in the valley and contest one another for possession of ewes. Their battles are brutal. On one quiet fall day, I heard the sound of two horned gladiators colliding. Scanning the slopes with my binoculars, I located the rams almost half a mile away.

Many Glacier Valley also serves as a jumping-off point for trails to a variety of interesting areas. One leads to Iceberg Lake, a turquoise-colored pendant almost always filled with floating ice chunks. Through the years I've heard wranglers tell people the lake is so cold that fish must grow fur to survive. Indeed!

The valley also offers a trail that leads to one of the park's two backcountry chalets. The trail is steep, passing through a variety of vegetative zones. In the course of a hike several hours long, visitors can accomplish what would take days if they were driving south to north over the flatland.

The trail to the chalet begins in a grove of aspens and passes through stands of spruce and fur. Ultimately it reaches a vegetative zone similar to the arctic alpine—the equivalent of driving 1,000 miles north.

Of all the vegetative zones, the arctic alpine is the harshest and probably the park's most fascinating. To thrive in a region where summers are but a few months long, both flora and fauna have had to make adaptations. For example, to help retard evaporation from the desiccating winds, plants have to be covered with fine hairlike structures or produce waxy leaves.

Hikers cross the moraine created by Grinnell Glacier with Salamander Glacier in the background.

Most arctic flowers also grow in clumps and are very low to the ground. Janie calls these flowers "belly plants" because she needs to scoot along the ground on her stomach to capture their beauty on film. This approach is suggested for others as well—only by observing flowers close-up can visitors appreciate the plants' delicate features.

Wildlife has also made special adaptations. Goats, for instance, grow thick fur, which is further covered by layers of long guard hairs.

Marmots have adapted to the park's harsh environment by hibernating almost nine months. But one of the most interesting adaptations is one made by the pika, a tiny member of the rabbit family that remains active year-round. Pikas are abundant near Swiftcurrent Pass, and as we approached the area we heard the tell-tale calls: *Kyack. Kyack.* Looking around we saw several pikas scurrying over a field of boulders, their mouths filled with grass. Walking toward them, we found bundles of grasses they'd left like so many piles of hay in the sun. Smart creatures! When snow accumulates, these dried-out piles of grass will serve as their winter larder.

From Many Glacier to Granite Park Chalet over Swiftcurrent Pass is a 7.5-mile hike. It's an uphill grind, and many hikers make reservations for both meals and sleeping accommodations. But day hikers are also welcome.

When we arrived at the chalet, a blustery wind had started blowing. Hot tea revitalized us, and soon everyone was chatting. Some had hiked in from Logan Pass along the Garden Wall Trail; others had ground out long miles, coming from Canada over Fifty Mountain. Most had seen goats and sheep, although none had seen bears.

A waitress told us that grizzlies had been seen several days ago through binoculars (the preferred way to encounter grizzlies) about a mile from the chalet. Bears fascinate everyone, and they certainly interested me. Through my work as a seasonal ranger, I've enjoyed more than seventy sightings. Before leaving I hoped to visit with several rangers and learn more about the park's evolving bear management program.

Many of my friends still work in the park, refusing transfers to higher pay-ing positions because of their love for Glacier. My former boss, Joe Ries, was now stationed at Two Medicine, and he invited us to visit. When we arrived, Ries was concerned about a lady who was lost. She had gone fishing with her husband but had decided to return because she thought her city shoes were inappropriate for hiking. A search party found her later in the day. She had taken a wrong turn on the trail. "Not much has changed," Ries said with a smile that evening.

With rangers, as with visitors, the most compelling conversations concern bears. Park rangers constantly exchange information over their two-way radios, noting visitors' observations and those of their own. Following a confirmed bear sighting, the location is logged on a map and entered into a computer. If a bear exhibits certain types of undesirable behavior, rangers close the area, use adverse conditioning, or remove the bear. Still, maulings occur.

Several weeks prior to our outing, two girls walking quietly had surprised a grizzly. Alarmed, the bear attacked but inflicted only puncture wounds and lac-erations. The girls walked out and were taken to the hospital.

Some believe Glacier may end up being the last home in the lower forty-eight states for the grizzly bear. As caretakers of a national park, Glacier per-sonnel have the responsibility of preserving this animal, a process best accomplished by separating man and grizzly. Managers believe that if visitors follow the suggestions outlined in park pamphlets, they have little to fear from the park's 300-plus grizzlies.

Glacier's bears have created legends, and one of the park's greatest stories occurred in Cut Bank Valley, the site of my old ranger station and a place of

Bighorn sheep in Many Glacier in late November often determine dominance by simply pawing and then assessing the response.

exquisite beauty. Driving into the valley, I pointed out mountains to Janie that reminded me of exciting times: Eagle Plume, White Calf, Medicine Grizzly—and the most conspicuous eastern mountain, Mad Wolf.

Mad Wolf was one of the most famous Native American orators, and in the late 1800s he spoke about a "Medicine Grizzly." According to his story, the spirit of a Flathead Indian chief had entered a huge grizzly. For years the reincarnated chief roamed Cut Bank Valley, exacting revenge against the Blackfeet for ambushing his fellow warriors and eventually killing his body—but not his spirit. Blackfeet believed in the reincarnation because the chief's medicine had been the grizzly, the most powerful and difficult to acquire.

About ten years ago I had ridden John, the park's horse, up Mad Wolf Mountain, attempting to chase wild horses out of the park. While I was there, a monster grizzly followed me briefly. The wind had been blowing from the bear toward me with all the fury of a gale-force storm, and the grizzly—which has poor vision—was curious. When I reined the horse, the bear scurried off, plowing through fields of glacier lilies and churning up sod—its muscles rippling. I gazed in awe, believing I had seen a descendant of the famous Medicine Grizzly. Now I was back and remembering my experiences at Mad Wolf.

Late that afternoon Janie and I forded a stream, passed through stands of ancient timber, and then broke out into a meadow, the same clearing where I'd once seen the giant bear. Nothing was there now other than shadows that played tricks with our imaginations. We moved close together and examined inky forms that assumed the primordial.

Engulfed by country shaped by fire, sculpted and chiseled by ice, anything seemed possible.

We stood awed.

A fawn tries to hide in Glacier National Park.

Chapter 2
Hiking Down the Park

My first introduction to Glacier National Park was back in the 1960s, shortly after I graduated from high school. Later I worked in the park on a blister rust control crew trying to save the white pine. White pine blister rust is a disease that was introduced from England, and its host is the gooseberry (*Ribes*). Spores from the gooseberry enter the stomata of white pine needles, descend through the food and water–conducting elements of the tree, and eventually enter the bark. With time the blister rust girdles the tree and kills it.

Certainly I remember those times. But more than that, I remember the weekends when we would hike Glacier's trails.

The following information is based on thirteen summers of work in Glacier. It is also based on the dozens of hikes and overnight trips Janie and I have made over the years. As an introduction to Glacier National Park, this guide cannot include all the hikes we have made (over the years I've hiked *every* GNP trail!). Instead we're offering some of the trips that have particularly moved us—a sampling of what Glacier has to offer.

Virtually everything in Glacier has its rewards, so be assured you'll derive soul-moving experiences from any of the other hikes, kayak trips, ski outings, and mountain climbs we offer here in abbreviated form. The key is repetition—repetition that allows for a variety of experiences from which you can then extract a philosophy for life. Glacier National Park offers that kind of magic. Use the foldout map to choose how to explore this incredible place even further.

Glacier offers a wonderful chance for you to acquire Native American perspectives about the park's history and its resources. Called "Native America Speaks," this program is very popular during the summer months. At St. Mary Visitor Center you'll find a Blackfeet tepee, indicating the park's commitment to the Blackfeet and Salish-Kootenai tribes and their contribution to Glacier in their offering of dancing, drumming, and songs. The visitor center and the tepee have more information on times and tickets for these fascinating summer programs.

Blackfeet participants, such as singer-poet Jack Gladstone with his "Legends of Glacier" and "Blackfeet Drumming and Dancing" with Joe McKay and Ray Croff, have been popular for many years.

We hope these suggestions help you acquire experiences that will eventually come to have the same meaning for you that they now have for us.

Glacier National Park fees are likely to change every year, but these are the parkwide entrance station fees as of 2007.

1 single person (a walker or biker, etc.)	$12 for 7 days
1 single vehicle	$25 for 7 days
Glacier Park pass	$35 for 1 year
National Parks pass	$80 for 1 year
Senior Pass (62 or older)	$10 for life

Over the years, the following trails have risen to the level of personal favorites. Although there are many more trails than what we've offered here, these will get you started—and will keep you going for a long, long time. For more details and for more trails, pick up a copy of *Hiking Glacier and Waterton Lakes National Parks* by Erik Molvar (The Globe Pequot Press). We've sorted these hikes by the park's various geographical locations, which are shown on the foldout map.

Many Glacier Region

Located on the east side of the park, the Many Glacier area contains remnants of some of the last visible glaciers as well as hikes that will take you into prime grizzly bear habitat.

To get to Many Glacier, take Going-to-the-Sun Road from West Glacier east to St. Mary. Then take U.S. Highway 89 north to Babb. At the Babb intersection, turn left (the road is signed TO MANY GLACIER) and go about 12 miles to the entrance gate. (An entrance fee is required.)

Grinnell Glacier

This 5.5-mile one-way hike climbs 1,600 feet to the Grinnell Glacier overlook to view a glacier that once extended yet another mile down the valley from its current location. The trail passes through prime grizzly bear habitat, and the overlook offers excellent opportunities to see bighorn sheep.

The trailhead begins at the picnic area near Swiftcurrent Lake or at the south end of Many Glacier Hotel. Take the signed trail, skirting the western shore of Swiftcurrent Lake; then go halfway around Lake Josephine to the signed trail leading to the glacier. Once at the glacier, you have a chance to address the subject of global warming. (See Global Warming Side Trip on page 26 for more on the subject). If you have time, join a hike conducted by a naturalist. This guided hike is a full-day trip, but naturalists have information

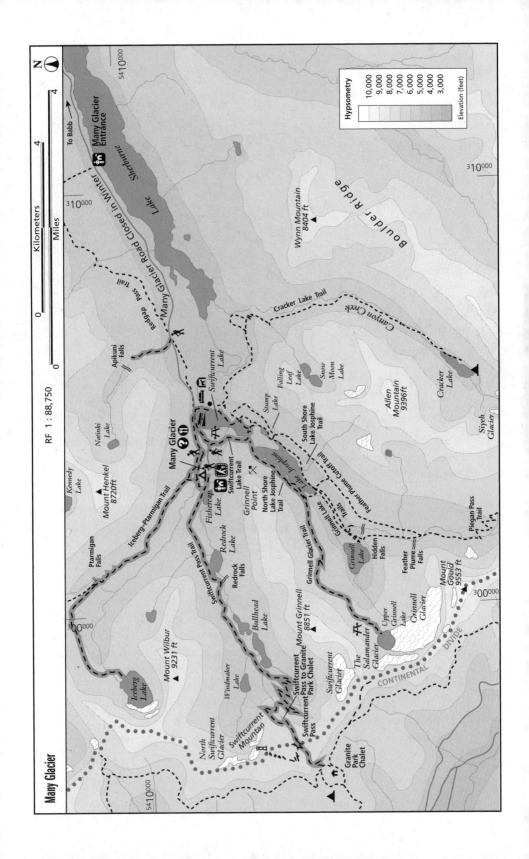

Many Glacier

RF 1 : 88,750

N

Hypsometry
- 10,000
- 9,000
- 8,000
- 7,000
- 6,000
- 5,000
- 4,000
- 3,000

Elevation (feet)

Kilometers

Miles

To Babb

Many Glacier Entrance

Many Glacier Road (Closed in Winter)

Redgap Pass Trail

Apikuni Falls

Lake Sherburne

Swiftcurrent Lake

Cracker Lake Trail

Canyon Creek

Wynn Mountain
8404 ft

Boulder Ridge

Natiniki Lake

Kennedy Lake

Mount Henkel
8720ft

Many Glacier

Iceberg-Ptarmigan Trail

Ptarmigan Falls

Swiftcurrent Pass Trail

Fishercap Lake

Redrock Lake

Redrock Falls

Grinnell Point

Swiftcurrent Lake Trail

North Shore Lake Josephine Trail

Stump Lake

Falling Leaf Lake

Snow Moon Lake

South Shore Lake Josephine Trail

Lake Josephine

Feather Plume Cutoff Trail

Allen Mountain
9396ft

Siyeh Glacier

Cracker Lake

Iceberg Lake

Mount Wilbur
9231 ft

Windmaker Lake

Bullhead Lake

Grinnell Glacier Trail

Grinnell Lake

Hidden Falls

Grinnell Lake Trails

Feather Plume Falls

Piegan Pass Trail

North Swiftcurrent Glacier

Swiftcurrent Mountain

Swiftcurrent Pass

Swiftcurrent Pass to Granite Park Chalet

Mount Grinnell
8851 ft

The Salamander Glacier

Upper Grinnell Lake

Grinnell Glacier

Mount Gould
9553 ft

Swiftcurrent Glacier

CONTINENTAL DIVIDE

Granite Park Chalet

There are discoveries to be made around every corner, as Dr. David Bristol learns when we stumble across rippled rock, part of an ancient shoreline.

acquired both from education and from experience answering questions posed by thousands of tourists.

Iceberg Lake

This 4.5-mile one-way hike climbs 1,200 feet to a lake that invariably contains ice throughout the summer. Jokesters like to tell novices that the lake is so cold that its waters contain furbearing fish, so be forewarned. The lake is located in an alpine setting, and during summer the area is carpeted with flowers also found in the tundra. Once David Shea, a ranger friend, encountered a grizzly here with a marmot firmly held in its jaws.

The Iceberg-Ptarmigan Trail departs from the north end of Swiftcurrent Lodge, near the cabins. Parking is available at the trailhead.

Bears frequent both sides of this trail, and summer wildflowers are gorgeous. At 2.3 miles you reach Ptarmigan Falls, a great place for rest and a picnic. Soon after the falls, the trail to Ptarmigan Tunnel comes in from the right; stay straight and you'll reach beautiful Iceberg Lake in another 2.2 miles.

Ptarmigan Tunnel

Ptarmigan Tunnel was completed in 1931 by the Civilian Conservation Corps (CCC) and provides wonderful views of the Belly River Drainage, an area all hard-core backpackers should see at least once. Departing Many Glacier, you start on the same trail as you would take to Iceberg Lake but split off to the right at about 2.5 miles. From here the trail climbs abruptly until you finally reach Ptarmigan Tunnel after a 5.2-mile one-way hike and a 2,300-foot climb.

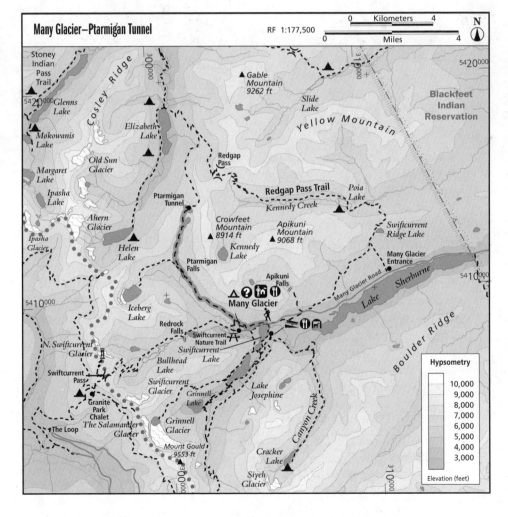

Grinnell Glacier continues to recede, having lost over 90 percent of the mass first seen in the 1880s (2003 photo).

Swiftcurrent Pass to Granite Park Chalet

This challenging 11.5-mile shuttle hike climbs 2,300 feet and then drops down to Granite Park Chalet and to the West Side Loop. This trip requires a shuttle or two vehicles. Start early and enjoy tea and cookies at the chalet. You can also spend the night at the chalet (about $75 per person; bring your own food and bedding) and then complete your hike the following day, returning either to Many Glacier or continuing on to the loop.

The trailhead is located at the west end of the parking lot for Swiftcurrent Lodge Restaurant and Coffee Shop.

Apikuni Falls

At only 2 miles in and out, this pretty hike on a good trail is a great family hike. The well-marked trailhead is located on the right on Many Glacier Road, at Mile 10.4 (coming from Babb).

Two Medicine Valley

From West Glacier take U.S. Highway 2 east to East Glacier. Take Highway 49 north for 4 miles to the sign on the left for Two Medicine. Go 9 miles on the paved road to the campground, ranger station, and snack bar. There is a fee entrance station on the road in. The roads into "Two Med" are closed in winter. Here you'll find a wonderful campground and access to more than a dozen different trails. The following are some of our favorites—and some are not easy.

Running Eagle Falls Nature Trail

This 0.3-mile loop is a good introduction to the area on a completely level trail to an interesting falls. Because water for the falls comes from both a deep crevasse and a stream, it once was called Trick Falls. However, in a wonderful renaming ceremony the name was changed to Running Eagle Falls in 1981, which is much more in keeping with the history of Native Americans in the area. Chief Earl Old Person from the local Blackfeet Indian Reservation attended the ceremony. The well-marked trailhead is 1 mile west of the entrance station. The trail is wheelchair accessible.

Dawson and Pitamakan Passes

You can make these difficult hikes together or individually since they can be reached independently of each other. The hike to Dawson Pass is 6.7 miles one way; the Pitamakan Pass hike is 6.9 miles one way. By combining the two hikes into an 18.8-mile loop, you add 5.2 miles to the total length without having to backtrack. It doesn't make much difference which direction you begin; both are equally difficult, climbing about 2,500 feet. Hiking this entire route has the added benefit of passing by Cut Bank Pass, once used by the Flathead Indians en route to buffalo hunting grounds in the prairies to the east. Because the hike already starts at a lofty elevation, you quickly climb above timberline and are continuously exposed to dramatic views, some of the most spectacular country in the park. This hike is highly recommended, but not for those with acrophobia.

The Dawson-Pitamakan trailhead is located on the north side of Two Medicine Campground at the outlet for Pray Lake. (Here it's called the Two Medicine North Shore trailhead.) To make the 18.8-mile loop, it makes no difference whether you hike clockwise or counterclockwise. To reach Dawson Pass *only*, hike west toward Twin Falls, where boat passengers can disembark and pick up the trail.

Scenic Point

This hike climbs 2,350 feet in 3.1 miles to Scenic Point. Begin at the Mount Henry trailhead, which is about 0.25 mile east of Two Medicine Ranger Station.

Two Medicine Valley

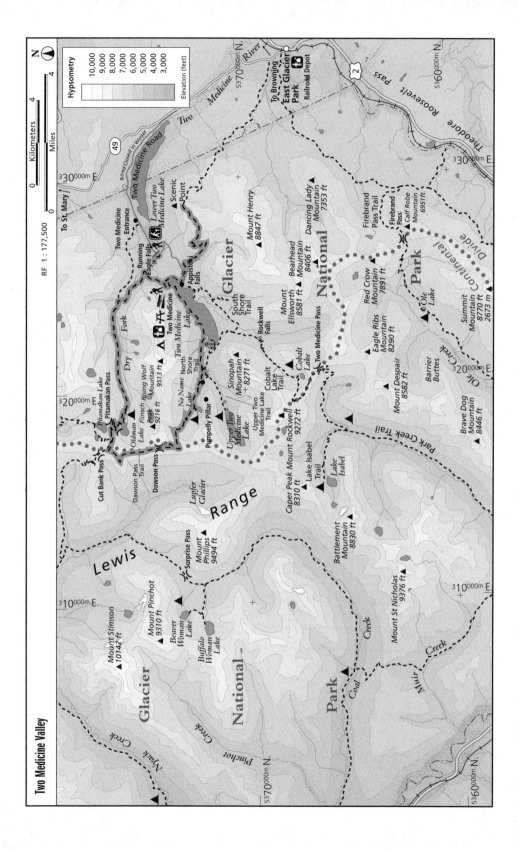

RF 1 : 177,500

Hypsometry

Elevation (feet)

10,000
9,000
8,000
7,000
6,000
5,000
4,000
3,000

Theodore Roosevelt Pass

To Browning

East Glacier Park

Railroad Depot

Two Medicine River

Firebrand Pass Trail

Firebrand Pass

Calf Robe Mountain 6951 ft

Continental Divide

Scenic Point

Mount Henry 8847 ft

Dancing Lady Mountain 7353 ft

Glacier

Two Medicine Entrance

Running Eagle Falls

Appistoki Falls

South Shore Trail

Bearhead Mountain 8581 ft

Red Crow Mountain 7891 ft

National

Summit Mountain 8770 ft 2673 m

Ole Lake

Ole Creek

Park

Two Medicine Road Road Closed in Winter

To St Mary

Lower Two Medicine Lake

Dry Fork

Two Medicine Lake

Rockwell Falls

Mount Ellsworth 8581 ft

Two Medicine Pass

Eagle Ribs Mountain 8290 ft

Mount Despair 8582 ft

Barrier Buttes

Brave Dog Mountain 8446 ft

Pitamakan Pass

Pitamakan Lake

Flinsch Peak 9513 ft

Rising Wolf Mountain 9216 ft

No Name Lake

North Shore Trail

Sinopah Mountain 8271 ft

Cobalt Lake

Cobalt Lake Trail

Cut Bank Pass

Oldman Lake

Pumpelly Pillar

Upper Two Medicine Lake

Upper Two Medicine Lake Trail

Caper Peak Mount Rockwell 9272 ft

Lake Isabel 8310 ft

Lake Isabel Trail

Park Creek Trail

Dawson Pass Trail

Dawson Pass

Lupfer Glacier

Range

Surprise Pass

Mount Phillips 9494 ft

Battlement Mountain 8830 ft

Mount St Nicholas 9376 ft

Lewis

Mount Stimson 10142 ft

Mount Pinchot 9310 ft

Beaver Woman Lake

Buffalo Woman Lake

Glacier

National

Park

Coal Creek

Muir Creek

Creek

Nyack Creek

Pinchot Creek

This hike is not for the out of shape! Try it if you're in reasonably good shape, but take your time—the reward of being able to look over the great sweep of plains is almost spiritual. From here either retrace your route or follow the well-marked trail through prime grizzly country back to East Glacier. The outstanding scenery never stops, and all you have to do is remember to make lots of noise, for this is prime bear habitat. Even with the bears, we firmly believe that you're safer on the trail than competing with summer traffic and gawking, inattentive tourists.

Appistoki Falls

This 1.2-mile in-and-out hike is a good leg stretcher for after dinner—or to tantalize you with what the longer hikes might offer. Take the Mount Henry Trail, located 0.25 mile east of the ranger station, and follow it for about 0.6 mile to a viewpoint, climbing about 260 feet.

St. Mary Region

In and around the area of St. Mary on the east side of the park are a number of Park Service and commercial campgrounds, all of which provide springboards to excellent hiking. The area contains about a dozen trails, and some are very easy, including Baring Falls, 0.3-mile one-way; Sun Point Nature Trail, 0.7-mile one-way; and Sunrift Gorge, a mere 200 feet one-way. In fall the area is loaded with bugling elk (check out the Two Dog Flats area about 2 miles southwest from the St. Mary Campground), making this an ideal time to visit. To reach the St. Mary area, take Going-to-the-Sun Road east from West Glacier for approximately 50 miles.

Siyeh Pass

Start your hike at the Piegan Pass trailhead (about 15 miles west of St. Mary), immediately adjacent to Siyeh Creek, and begin a gradual climb of about 2.5 miles to Preston Park with its multitude of summer flowers. Here the trail splits, with the left fork going to Piegan Pass and the right fork to Siyeh Pass. From Preston Park you can also see to the top of Going-to-the-Sun Peak, which once served as a site for Native American vision quests. The peak may well serve as the final resting place for a friend of ours who climbed this peak in 1962, signed the log, but was never seen again.

Climb another 2 miles to Siyeh Pass and then eat lunch, sit, nap, or simply bask in the beauty of a commanding view of almost 360 degrees. From here you can look out over the prairie in one direction and back toward Logan Pass with its lofty peaks. Of course you're already sitting on a lofty peak, but believe me, don't fear that you'll become jaded—everything is grand, just in a different way. When your time starts running out, pick yourself up and proceed down past

Chief Earl Old Person spoke at the ceremony changing the name from Trick Falls to Running Eagle Falls in 1981.

Sexton Glacier and then toward Baring Falls for a total of about 12 miles. From here you'll need to hike up to your car (now about 4 miles away), hitchhike, or team up for a shuttle. This is not an easy hike, but the promise of beauty stacked on beauty with each new stream, each new patch of flowers, each new sighting

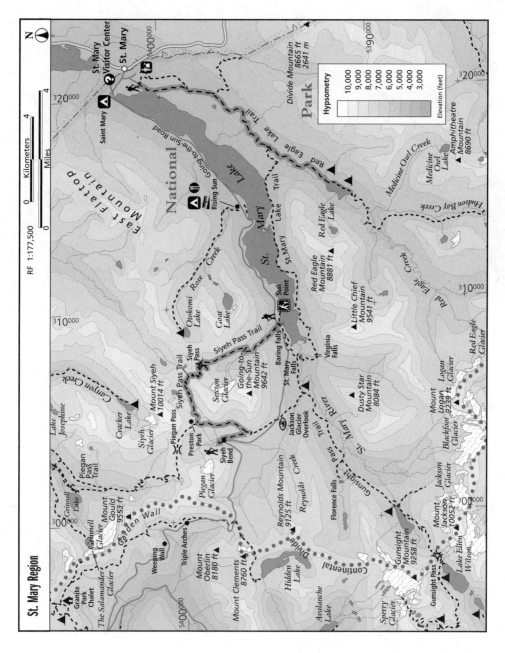

The scenery of St. Mary Valley is breathtakingly beautiful year-round.

of wildlife, seems to spur hikers on to complete the 2,240-foot climb to Siyeh Pass.

Red Eagle Lake

A total of 15.2 miles out and back, the Red Eagle Lake hike offers beauty along the way and good fishing upon arrival. The climb is only 200 feet, but the length of the hike classifies it as moderate. Unless you have lots of energy, plan to camp at the lake (check at the visitor center for campsite availability and get a backcountry permit; both campsites are primitive).

The huge Red Eagle Fire of 2006 caused extensive damage to this area. Approximately 19,186 acres burned in the park section of the Red Eagle area along with an additional 15,000 acres on the adjacent Blackfeet Reservation. Some of the beautiful Douglas firs and lodgepole pines survived the inferno.

Fire is part of the natural process in the park. It changes habitats and affects many creatures and various types of flora. The bears may not return for a while, but woodpeckers and other birds will reestablish themselves. Some, in fact, will find these conditions more suitable than the prefire conditions. The new growth will revegetate quickly and will do so in very predictable stages until eventually a "climax" species reforests the area.

The trailhead for Red Eagle is located at the Old Ranger Station parking area. From the St. Mary Visitor Center (going west), take the paved road to the right, which is just a couple of hundred yards beyond the center, and follow it to the parking lot and marked trailhead. For a large portion of the hike, you'll parallel St. Mary Lake, with lots of pretty views. The trail ascends and descends through the old woods and meadows, crossing several swinging bridges, until you emerge at the lake. Don't forget your camera and fishing pole.

Logan Pass

Named for the park's first superintendent, William Logan, Logan Pass is the apex of a 50-mile drive along the Going-to-the-Sun Road. At 6,646 feet above sea level, the pass is already so high that you don't have to do much to find unparalleled vistas. By simply parking in the visitor center lot or walking to the visitor center, you can have a commanding view of peaks such as Bishop's Cap, Mount Gould, Heavy Runner (named after the chief killed in the infamous Baker Massacre), Mount Clements, and Reynolds Peak. From the right perspective you even can see to the Great Plains. The hike to Hidden Lake is a must because it provides unparalleled opportunities to see wildlife. In fact, this is one of the few places in the park where I've seen weasels.

Hidden Lake

Hike 1.5 miles to the Hidden Lake overlook and we can virtually guarantee that if you keep your eyes open, you'll see marmots and goats. On exceptional days look out to your left (as you climb) and you may well see a grizzly sweeping up clods of dirt as it tries to unearth the bulbs of glacier lilies. From the Hidden Lake overlook, you'll see a sheet of turquoise-colored water, backdropped by Bear Hat Mountain, an imposing peak. Add another 1.5 miles down to the lake (it's rather a grind coming back up) for a total round-trip of 6 miles. The trailhead is located at the Logan Pass Visitor Center.

Granite Park Chalet

There are two trails to Granite Park Chalet on Glacier's west side. Take the Loop Trail (about 7 miles west of Logan Pass, with a small parking lot) for a 4-mile one-way hike to the chalet, climbing 2,200 feet. Or access the Highline Trail on the north side of Going-to-the-Sun Road directly across from the Logan Pass Visitor Center. This 7.6-mile one-way hike climbs 200 feet. We've

The Highline Trail departs from Logan Pass and heads toward Granite Park Chalet, about 8 miles.

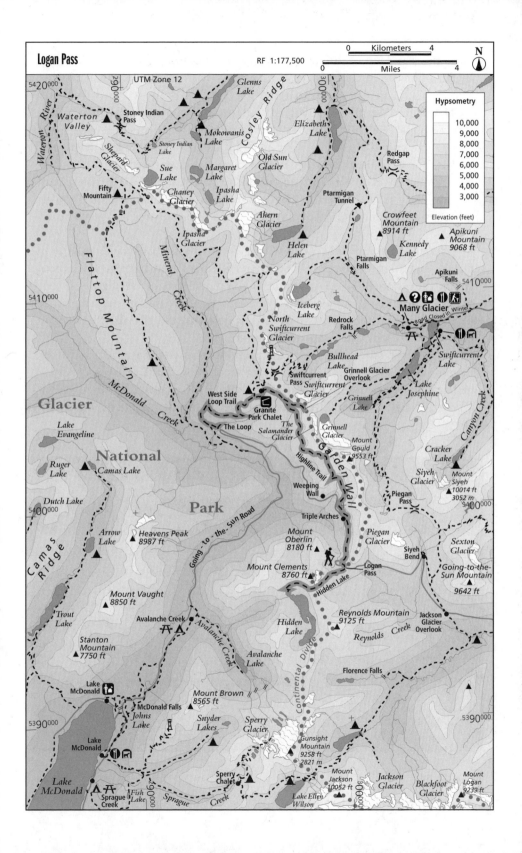

made this trip dozens of times, hiking the 7.6 miles from Logan Pass to Granite Park Chalet and then 4 miles down to the West Side Loop. (You'll need to shuttle cars if you choose this route.)

Departing Logan Pass, at about 3 miles from the pass, the Highline Trail climbs up Haystack Butte, an area where bands of bighorns typically hang out in the summer in bachelor herds. From Granite Park Chalet the trail drops into timbered areas of the park where fires have sprung up and been put down, but not without weeks of work. As you descend to the West Side Loop, you're also looking out at Heaven's Peak, a great nontechnical mountain to climb if you're young, in shape, and know the route. Make this 11.6-mile trek and you'll never regret it.

Global Warming Side Trip: Hiking from Logan Pass, you'll come to a fork in the trail that is about 0.75 mile from Granite Park Chalet. A sign directs you to the Grinnell Glacier overlook. If you're interested in seeing the effects of global warming, take the path. Log on to www.nrmsc.usgs.gov/repeatphoto/ gg_mt-gould.htm for the stunning photos below of the glacial changes. You might want to print out a copy to bring with you.

Hike to the overlook, extract the printout from your day pack, and then examine the change. The 1938 Hileman photograph shows that Upper Grinnell Lake did not exist at this time. The 1981 USGS photo, however, shows Upper Grinnell Lake and reveals that half the area is now ice and the other half

Grinnell Glacier from Mt. Gould
1938 - 2006

1938
Hileman photo
GNP Archives

1981
Key photo
USGS

1998
Fagre photo
USGS

2006
Holzer photo
USGS

is glacial melt. Seventeen years later, in 1998, Dr. Dan Fagre's photo shows the lake still contains about 25 percent ice, but the 2006 USGS photo shows the lake devoid of ice and that Upper Grinnell Lake is now firmly established—all in the course of fifty years. In 1850 the park hosted 150 substantial glaciers. Dr. Fagre, a global-warming expert, says that by the year 2030, all the park's remaining twenty-seven glaciers will be gone. As a World Heritage Site, Glacier National Park is providing the world with many answers to global warming; Grinnell Lake provides but one manifestation. Park interpreters will discuss the topic of climate change during summer talks.

Cut Bank Valley

This is one of my favorite areas; I worked out of this east-side ranger station for several years. The valley is steeped in Indian lore and recalls the now historic feats enacted by both Native Americans and early-day rangers. Here's where Mad Wolf encountered the famous Medicine Grizzly. Here's where the Blackfeet and Flathead engaged in a historic conflict. And here's where Chance Beebe, one of the park's first rangers, began reducing predators—the policy practiced during those times. Appropriately, surrounding mountains carry such names as Eagle Plume, Mad Wolf, Medicine Grizzly Peak, and Medicine Owl. We love this area and suggest that you camp for at least a few days in this seldom-visited place.

To reach the Cut Bank Valley, go north from East Glacier for 13 miles on Highway 49 to Kiowa Junction. Take US 89 north for about 6 miles to the signed turnoff on the left (west) side of the road into Cut Bank. This last dirt road is closed in winter.

Medicine Grizzly Lake

A 6-mile one-way hike goes through timber to a lake that from time to time offers good fishing and wonderful scenery. As you hike you'll parallel Cut Bank Creek part of the way.

The Medicine Grizzly Lake Trail begins from a small parking lot just beyond the Cut Bank Ranger Station. From the trail sign you'll follow the north fork of Cut Bank Creek. At a junction in 1 mile, keep to the right for the lake. At 3.9 miles, stay to the right at another signed junction. At Mile 4.6 turn left for the lake, which you'll reach in another 1.4 miles.

Triple Divide Peak

I once climbed this peak with Senator Max Baucus. You begin this hike as though you were going to Medicine Grizzly Lake, but at Mile 4.6 take the right fork up to Triple Divide Pass, climbing the north side of Atlantic Creek Valley. If you plan to proceed from here to Triple Divide Peak, you should first

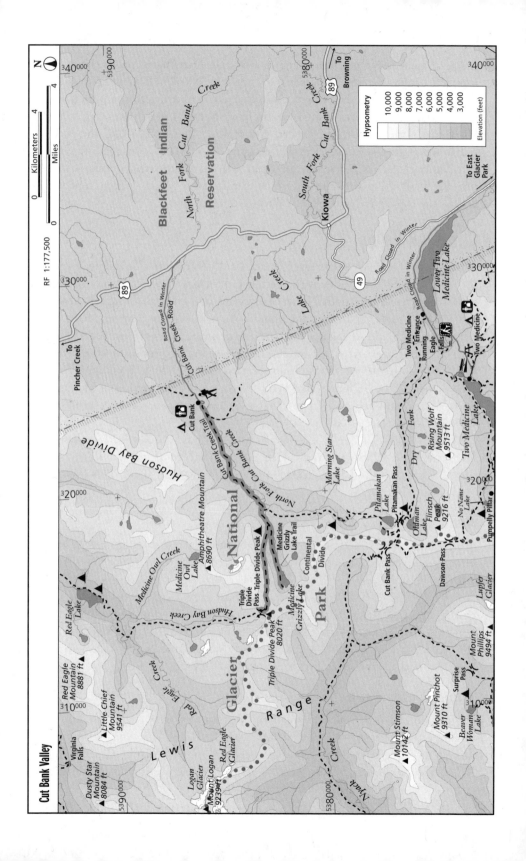

Cut Bank Valley

RF 1:177,500

Hypsometry

| 10,000 |
| 9,000 |
| 8,000 |
| 7,000 |
| 6,000 |
| 5,000 |
| 4,000 |
| 3,000 |

Elevation (feet)

Kilometers

Miles

N

Blackfeet   Indian

Reservation

North Fork   Cut Bank   Creek

South Fork Cut Bank Creek

Kiowa

To Browning

Road Closed in Winter

To East Glacier Park

Lower Two Medicine Lake

Two Medicine Lake

Two Medicine Entrance

Running Eagle Falls

Two Medicine

Rising Wolf Mountain 9513 ft

Dry Fork

No Name Lake

Pumpelly Pillar

Flinsch Peak 9216 ft

Oldman Lake

Pitamakan Pass

Pitamakan Lake

Dawson Pass

Cut Bank Pass

Lupfer Glacier

Mount Phillips 9494 ft

Surprise Pass

Mount Pinchot 9310 ft

Beaver Woman Lake

Mount Stimson 10142 ft

Nyack

Creek

Triple Divide Peak 8020 ft

Red Eagle Glacier

Logan Glacier

Mount Logan 9239 ft

Red Eagle Creek

Little Chief Mountain 9541 ft

Red Eagle Mountain 8881 ft

Red Eagle Lake

Dusty Star Mountain 8084 ft

Virginia Falls

Lewis   Range

Glacier

Park

National

Continental   Divide

Hudson Bay Creek

Medicine Grizzly Lake

Triple Divide Pass

Triple Divide Peak 8690 ft

Medicine Grizzly Lake Trail

Medicine Owl Lake

Amphitheatre Mountain

Medicine Owl Creek

Hudson Bay Divide

Cut Bank Creek Trail

Morning Star Lake

Cut Bank

Cut Bank Creek Road

Road Closed in Winter

To Pincher Creek

Creek

Lake

49

89

89

acquaint yourself with the route by reading J. Gordon Edwards's *A Climber's Guide to Glacier National Park* and have a good topo map. Triple Divide is 7.2 miles from the trailhead at Cut Bank Ranger Station, and the elevation gain is 2,380 feet. If you're acquainted with the flow of continental waters, then you'll understand one reason for climbing this peak. Pour a little water from your water bottle onto the peak of this mountain—and watch as it splits into three and begins its subsequent flow to the three main watersheds: the Atlantic and Pacific Oceans and Canada's Hudson Bay.

Lake McDonald Valley

Like many other areas of the park, this valley takes its name from a historic figure, in this case Duncan McDonald, who explored this area when he freighted supplies to Canada. Although there are many trails here—and all are interesting—most don't have the drama of their namesake. Lake McDonald is the largest body of water in the park. Eagles and loons are often spotted around the lake.

Avalanche Lake

This is one of the few trails on which we've seen a mountain lion or cougar. It was in winter on a cross-country ski trip, and the cat was hot in pursuit of a small group of elk. The lake itself is a destination, for it parallels one of the most beautiful gorges in the park. The signed trail begins from the east side of Going-to-the-Sun Road, about 6 miles north from the north end of the lake near the campground entrance, and passes through a stately cedar-hemlock stand—some of the few that survived the fire of 1910. From here the trail steadily ascends for 2 miles to Avalanche Lake, climbing about 500 feet. The hike totals 4.2 miles to the foot of the lake and back and 5.8 miles to the head of the lake and back. The lake sits in an ancient cirque, and the waters resemble a turquoise-colored gem.

Trail of the Cedars

A wheelchair-accessible nature trail, the Trail of the Cedars is a lovely, flat 0.7-mile loop. You'll wander on a boardwalk and through a stately grove of cedar trees—the only place in the park where you'll find such trees.

The trailhead shares access with Avalanche Lake Trail. Start from the picnic area of Avalanche Campground, located about 6 miles north from the north end of Lake McDonald.

Huckleberry Mountain Lookout

This is perhaps one of the best places in the park to see grizzly bears on a consistent basis. One evening as we were descending, we counted five different

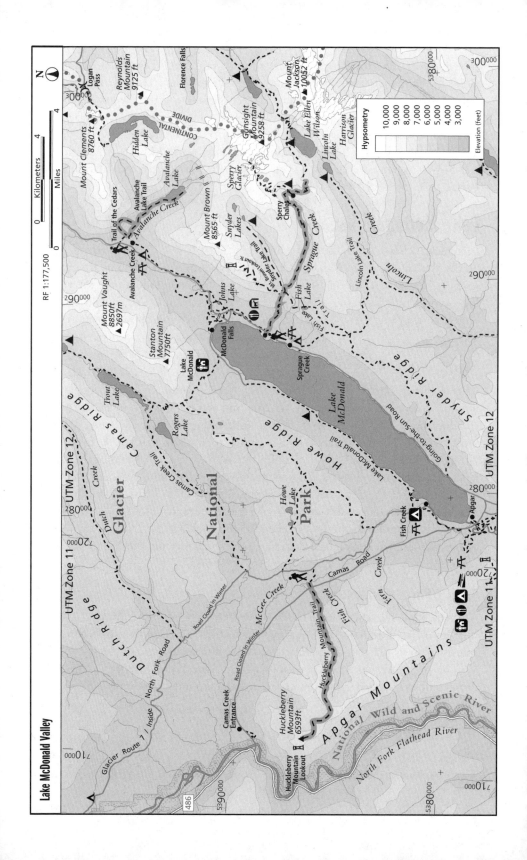

Lake McDonald Valley

RF 1:177,500

Hypsometry

Elevation (feet)
10,000
9,000
8,000
7,000
6,000
5,000
4,000
3,000

Logan Pass

Reynolds Mountain 9125 ft

Florence Falls

Mount Clements 8760 ft

CONTINENTAL DIVIDE

Hidden Lake

Gunsight Mountain 9258 ft

Mount Jackson 10052 ft

Lake Ellen Wilson

Lincoln Lake

Harrison Glacier

Avalanche Lake Trail

Avalanche Creek

Avalanche Lake

Sperry Glacier

Sperry Chalet

Sprague Creek

Lincoln Creek

Lincoln Lake Trail

Trail of the Cedars

Mount Brown 8565 ft

Snyder Lakes

Mt. Brown Lookout Tr.

Snyder Lake Trail

Fish Lake

Fish Lake Trail

Avalanche Creek

Mount Vaught 8850 ft 2697m

Stanton Mountain 7750 ft

Johns Lake

McDonald Falls

Lake McDonald

Sprague Creek

Lake McDonald

Lincoln

Trout Lake

Rogers Lake

Howe Ridge

Lake McDonald Trail

Going-to-the-Sun Road

Snyder Ridge

Camas Ridge

Dutch Creek

Glacier

Howe Lake

National

Park

Fish Creek

Apgar

UTM Zone 12

Camas Creek Trail

80°00'

720°00'

UTM Zone 11

UTM Zone 12

Dutch Ridge

Road Closed in Winter

North Fork Road

Camas Road

McGee Creek

Fish Creek

Fern Creek

UTM Zone 11

720°00'

Road Closed in Winter

Glacier Route 7 / Inside

Huckleberry Mountain Trail

Apgar Mountains

Camas Creek Entrance

Huckleberry Mountain 6593 ft

Huckleberry Mountain Lookout

North Fork Flathead River

National Wild and Scenic River

486

5390000

710°00'

5380000

5380000

5390000

300000

290°00'

280°00'

710°00'

Scale

Kilometers: 0 — 4

Miles: 0 — 4

N

bears in forty-five minutes. We were accompanied by the summer fire lookout, a crazed soul who encouraged us to proceed quietly so that we might see more bears. Needless to say, we proceeded in one fashion, he in another. The trail stretches 6 miles one-way and climbs 2,725 feet. To access the trailhead, take Camas Creek Road north from Apgar for about 6 miles to the signed trailhead on the left (west).

Sperry Chalet

Mostly through timber, this 6.4-mile one-way trail climbs 3,432 feet. Generally the rewards of this hike await you at the chalet, when you reach a congenial crew that provides great hospitality for guests, whether they are of the day or night variety. For an incredible experience, spend the night. In the morning, make the additional hike to Sperry Glacier, completing your return to your car on the second day. The trailhead is located on the east side of Going-to-the-Sun Road, across from the Lake McDonald Lodge entrance.

North Fork Area

Mostly timbered, the North Fork is rich in Glacier history—and now in wolves, which you might hear should you camp at either Bowman or Kintla Lake. Bert worked as a ranger one summer at Kintla; his experiences were great and his memories are keen. Once he saw a moose swimming the lake, and here's one of the other two places where he saw a mountain lion, this time poised over a deer kill. Kintla is also a wonderful lake on which to kayak, as is Bowman. Although the area offers many trails, we suspect most hikers will seek other trails offering greater vistas. Therefore, we suggest just one trail in this area: Numa Ridge Lookout.

The North Fork area may be accessed in several ways.

From Apgar Visitor Center in West Glacier, take the signed Camas Creek Road north for 11 miles to the junction with the Outside North Fork Road. Turn right on this road and go 16 miles to the settlement of Polebridge.

From Columbia Falls, take County Road 486 (also the North Fork Road) from the north side of town for approximately 37 miles to Polebridge. Just north of Polebridge, access the signed Bowman Creek Road; it's a 6-mile trip on a dirt road to the lake, the ranger station, and the trailhead for Numa Ridge Lookout. Park at the picnic area.

Numa Ridge Lookout

Those who are familiar with the works of Edward Abby will want to see one of the lookouts that stimulated his imagination—Numa Ridge Lookout. The trailhead is located at the Bowman Lake Ranger Station; from here the trail

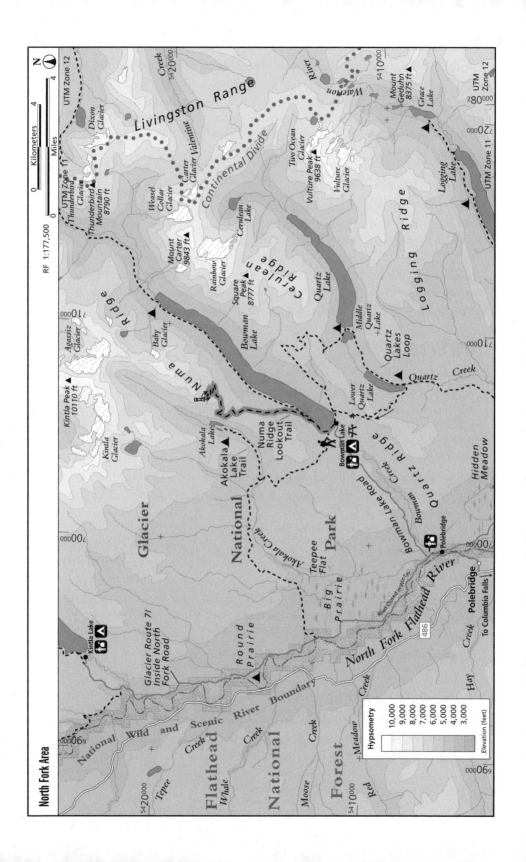

North Fork Area

RF 1:177,500

N

Kilometers
0   4
Miles
0   4

Livingston Range

Dixon
Glacier

Carter
Glacier Valentine

Thunderbird
Glacier

Thunderbird
Mountain
8790 ft

Weasel
Collar
Glacier

Continental Divide

Cerulean
Lake

Rainbow
Glacier

Mount
Carter
9843 ft

Square
Peak
8777 ft

Cerulean Ridge

Two Ocean
Glacier

Vulture Peak
9638 ft

Vulture
Glacier

Quartz
Lake

Waterton
River

Mount
Geduhn
8375 ft

Grace
Lake

Logging
Lake

Logging   Ridge

Middle
Quartz
Lake

Quartz
Lakes
Loop

Lower
Quartz
Lake

Quartz   Creek

Baby
Glacier

Agassiz
Glacier

Numa   Ridge

Kintla Peak
10110 ft

Kintla
Glacier

Bowman
Glacier

Bowman
Lake

Akokala
Lake

Akokala
Lake
Trail

Numa
Ridge
Lookout
Trail

Bowman Lake

Quartz   Ridge

Hidden
Meadow

Polebridge

Bowman Lake Road

Bowman Creek

Akokala Creek

Teepee
Flat Park

Big
Prairie

Glacier

National

Park

Glacier Route 71
Inside North
Fork Road

Kintla Lake

Round   Prairie

National   Wild   and   Scenic   River   Boundary

Flathead

National

Forest

Road Closed in Winter

North Fork Flathead River

486

Polebridge

Hay   Creek

To Columbia Falls

Tepee

Whale   Creek

Moose   Creek

Red

Meadow   Creek

Meadow

Creek

Hypsometry

10,000
9,000
8,000
7,000
6,000
5,000
4,000
3,000

Elevation (feet)

UTM Zone 12

UTM Zone 11

UTM Zone 11

UTM Zone 12

UTM Zone 11

Two kids romp near Logan Pass.

proceeds for 6.0 miles while climbing about 2,900 feet. In summer the Glacier Institute offers excursions to the lookout. Although they mention Abby's tenure here, the purpose of the excursions is to provide lessons on fire ecology, for the trail climbs through recent and extensive burns. From the lookout, you'll have great views of Square Peak, Mount Carter, the Whitefish Range across the North Fork, and north to Akokala Peak.

Glacier Prime

Those in the know—that is, Montana natives—suggest visiting the following areas in the park as prime examples of what the area has to offer, especially if you have several days to explore: Apgar, Avalanche Lake, Trail of the Cedars, Lake McDonald, Logan Pass, Garden Wall, Hidden Lake, Many Glacier Valley, Iceberg Lake, Grinnell Glacier Trail, Two Medicine Valley, and Running Eagle Falls.

If your time is limited to only a day or so, begin with the two- to three-hour drive over Going-to-the-Sun Road. Take the time to stop at pull-outs so that you can view one of the most amazing and beautiful mountain roads in the world. You can hike the three short nature trails along this road, beginning on the west side with the Trail of the Cedars. Hidden Lake Trail departs from behind the Logan Pass Visitor Center. Continue then toward St. Mary Lake and walk the Sun Point Nature Trail, which begins 9 miles west of St. Mary.

Glacier Cycling

Going-to-the-Sun Road

This highway, one of two major roads through Glacier National Park, is one of the most popular bike routes in the Northwest. However, it is also a popular motorway; the road is fairly narrow, so use caution. Also, portions of the route are closed to bikes for several hours each day. Check at the Apgar Ranger Station for closure schedules. Weekdays are probably better times to ride this road.

The moderate to advanced route is 56.5 miles long if you ride northeast from Apgar to St. Mary. Of course nothing says you have to do the entire route. But try to make it to Logan Pass, where you'll ride through some awesome scenery.

Take US 2 from Columbia Falls into West Glacier (there is an entrance fee for bikers) and follow the signs to Apgar Village, where you can park. Then hop on and go for it!

Polebridge to Kintla Lake

An easy to moderate mountain bike ride of 29 miles out and back, this trek takes you through some awesome scenery in the most northwestern part of Glacier National Park. Consider hauling camping gear—when you reach Kintla Lake (at 14.5 miles), you're probably going to want to stay awhile.

To reach Polebridge, take the North Fork Road (CR 486) from Columbia Falls and travel 38 miles to the town of Polebridge, where you begin your ride. Most of the North Fork Road is not paved and can be a bit rough. You can park at Polebridge, a wonderful, tiny community with a restaurant and general store. Head north out of Polebridge, following what is called the Inside North Fork Road until you reach Kintla Lake.

Mount Reynolds as seen from near the Logan Pass visitor center

If hiking is not in your plans, guided boat cruises are available on Lake McDonald, St. Mary Lake, and Two Medicine Lake and on Swiftcurrent Lake in Many Glacier. From the water you'll get an entirely different perspective of the park.

Our hiking friend Tom Richards departs from Granite Park Chalet with Heaven's Peak in the background.

The grizzly bear is omnivorous, feeding on plants, insects, and other animals. There is plenty for bears to eat in Glacier National Park; you don't need to feed them. Bears that associate humans with food can become dangerous and may have to be killed.

Chapter 3
Accessing the Burn Areas

On the night of July 23, 2003, those standing near the shores of Lake McDonald in Glacier National Park witnessed a ferocious aspect of nature created by the Robert Fire. When the wind gusted, 300-foot walls of flame stabbed the night sky. When the wind subsided, the smoke settled—and that may have been even more disconcerting.

Naturalist Doug Follett, a man I've known from my thirteen summers as a seasonal ranger, beginning in the late 1960s, said that although Lake McDonald was only 100 yards from the Apgar Visitor Center, you couldn't see it even in broad daylight. "We told visitors to walk north and that they'd know they'd reached the lake when their feet got wet," said Follet.

This million-acre park was sculpted so very long ago by massive glaciers. The effects of these glaciers are evident everywhere and serve as a backdrop for hundreds of species of plants. In turn, the plants provide forage for deer, elk, moose, and of course for the bighorn sheep and mountain goats that navigate the park's craggy peaks. At the top of the heap are the 300-plus grizzlies that strike awe in all visitors driving the famed Going-to-the-Sun Road or striding along some segment of the park's 700 miles of maintained trails.

But what has happened to these cherished and much-anticipated features of Glacier following the recent massive conflagrations? Will the park be little more than a blackened wasteland should they return? Has all the wildlife disappeared? Or can we expect a better scenario?

According to Glacier's fire specialist, Mitch Burgard, the quick answer can be summarized with a pronounced nod of optimism. Burgard says that old internal tree scars show that fires have always played a role in the area's ecology. But the fires of 2003 were the worst in the park's history, which dates back to 1910. "Vegetation may not yet be abundant," Burgard told me, "but watch what happens over the course of the next few years. Because so many different fires have burned near here in the historic past, the park staff has implemented programs and will be conducting interpretive hikes through the burned areas. West Glacier provides an excellent place not only to participate in those activities but also to embark on explorations of your own."

In fall 2004, after most of the fires had been contained, Janie and I began our exploration by camping at Fish Creek Campground. Apgar is another nearby campground, and both are located just a few miles past the West Glacier

Vegetation regrows after a fire along the North Fork Road.

entrance. If these campgrounds are full, there's a beautiful KOA located 5 miles south of Glacier's west entrance off U.S. Highway 2.

Using the West Glacier area as our base, we first drove several miles north of West Glacier along US 2, stopping at an overlook that gazed back over the park and over the area of the 1910 fire. The fire reduced dense vegetation, and within a few years this hillside became an ideal habitat for large mammals. Look along the steep banks on the far side of the Middle Fork; with patience you might very well see deer, elk, and bighorn sheep, as we did.

Back in the park, the Apgar and Fish Creek Campgrounds are within a short walk of Lake McDonald. Here you'll get a commanding view of the infamous Robert Fire, which burned right down to the lake's shores. From the Apgar Campground you can walk to the visitor center (still intact) from which thousands viewed the 2003 fires. Lake McDonald is just 100 yards from the campground. You can wet your feet, look across the mile-wide lake, and see the masses of trees downed by the Robert Fire. Over the past one hundred years, Glacier's five fires have consumed 145,880 acres of vegetation, or about 15 percent of the park. At the height of fire activity, 2,500 firefighters battled park-wide flames, ringing up a staggering cost of $99 million.

By itself, the Robert Fire consumed 57,570 acres and sometimes burned at a temperature of 2,100 degrees. You can observe the effects up close and personal from near the Fish Creek Campground just off Camas Creek Road. Follow a trail from the picnic area to the shores of Lake McDonald. As you walk, pay attention to your surroundings. Heat that scorched treetops also burrowed into the roots and weakened them. Because even the slightest of breezes could topple these trees onto unsuspecting hikers, the park closed all burned areas. Early winter snows and heavy December winds, however, knocked down many of the snags, and in January the park reopened the burned areas—cautioning hikers to remain vigilant. When we hiked last summer, we did so carefully and were surprised to see that new vegetation was already returning.

The West Glacier area also provides access to many other fire areas, and exploring them can be both exciting and instructive. One such "museum" is located about 5 miles up the Camas Creek Road at the Huckleberry Mountain Nature Trail. Although called a nature trail, the path really interprets the fire of 1967—showing with signs and a brochure just how much nature can repair itself in a few brief decades.

Immediately after a fire, certain species of vegetation are geared to respond. One such species is the lodgepole pine, which produces a type of cone—called a serotinous cone—that opens only when exposed to heat. Covering the cone is a hard waxy substance that melts after exposure to heat, thereby freeing the seed.

Standing along the trail, I recalled just how intense the heat had been years ago. As a seasonal ranger, I was involved in the 1967 fire and was driving a service vehicle along the Camas Creek Road. Suddenly, wind swelled, kicking up flames that "ran." In a matter of seconds flames swept over the road, almost engulfing me. For a few seconds, I knew fear that could paralyze. It was my first encounter with fire of that magnitude, and it provided an unparalleled experience about fire's power.

Leaving the nature trail, we returned to our vehicle, proceeded through the Camas Creek Road entrance station, and picked up the North Fork Road. Then we drove a few miles to the Big Creek Nature Center, a part of the Glacier Institute.

On the day of our visit, Jami Belt, the center's program director at the time, was explaining the role of natural fire using an arrangement of lit matches mounted in a type of pegboard. By varying the "density" of matches, Belt explained how fire acts as a thinning agent and, therefore, as a fire inhibitor. Because of so much public interest in fires, the center continues to offer courses on the topic. One of the courses will include hikes to the Numa Ridge and Apgar fire lookouts, both located in the national park. The course, entitled "A

Century of Fire History from the View of a Fire Lookout," will detail the role of fire but will also explain the historic role of lookouts in the park. To facilitate your visit, the Big Creek Center provides a campground just across the road, placing the facility within less than a five-minute walk from your campsite.

From Big Creek the road north passes sites where fires burned in 1910, 1967, 1988, 2001, and 2003. In some of the areas, new and dense forests of lodgepole pines stand like an impenetrable wall. Twenty miles later you'll arrive at the metropolis of Polebridge, population about fifty, with its famous Polebridge Mercantile and Northern Lights Saloon. Because fire has figured in the lives of these people so prominently, Dan and Deb Kaufmann of the Mercantile have posted a series of dramatic pictures on the wall of the store, presenting another vignette on the power of fire. In the past twenty years, fire has almost engulfed this community on three separate occasions, and memories are vivid.

Continuing past Polebridge along the 2-mile road into Glacier's North Fork entrance, we came to stand after stand of trees, but this time they were dead ones. These snags resulted from the fire of 1988, and they present another lesson on the effect of fire. Judging from the thousands of holes, insects had invaded these trees. In turn, woodpeckers and several species of owls sought out the insects.

Several years ago, Jami Belt had been part of a saw-whet owl survey. Using a proven technique, we followed her example and banged on the side of an old snag using a solid stick. Within an hour, the head of our subject of investigation popped from the hole, curious and not really alarmed. Though saw-whets can exist other places, like a variety of other bird species, they are attracted to such trees because of the insect life.

The presence of the owl and the rapid return to a forested land brought to mind a quote we had heard on a nature walk program with naturalist Doug Follett. Follett recalled that John Keats had once written, "The poetry of the earth is never dead."

Although such thoughts can sometimes assume a harsh aspect of nature, here in Glacier it also has a kinder, more gentle side—one we look forward to exploring beginning each spring.

Chapter 4
Climb the Good Mountains

John Muir advised us to "Climb the mountains and get their good tidings." As a further inducement he further suggested, "Nature's peace will flow into you as sunshine flows into trees. The winds will blow their own freshness into you, and the storms their energy, while cares will drop off like autumn leaves."

His advice is good, and Glacier National Park contains dozens of mountains that can be climbed. Over the years I've climbed many, including Triple Divide, Heaven's Peak, Mount Gould, Mad Wolf, Chief Mountain, and Mount Stimpson. None required technical skills, just good route-finding capabilities. I've often accompanied people who had climbed them before, benefiting from their knowledge—and from their mistakes.

If you want to climb mountains, you'll need to do some homework, acquiring more information than we have provided here in our essays suggesting why we climb. There's nothing else quite like it. If you're inspired, purchase J. Gordon Edwards's *A Climber's Guide to Glacier National Park* and detailed (1:63 360) maps. Most of all, make sure you're in shape to undertake an activity that can only be described as rigorous and, as you'll see, unpredictable. Use my experiences as a testimonial that you must assemble everything you need to endure the unexpected.

Chief Mountain Beguiles: Fickle Mountain Demands Respect

Its weather patterns help make Chief Mountain—a giant monolith located along the eastern edge of Glacier National Park—appear to be such an imposing and intriguing structure. On some days the mountain is backdropped by azure skies; on others it is shrouded in clouds and then swirled by winds that screech like a predatory bird.

Such is the manner by which our party of four men saw the mountain as we left our vehicle and began the climb along a well-marked trail, passing up through a thin veil of fog to the mountain's base. Suddenly we broke through the mist, and before us loomed Chief Mountain.

Clouds circled the Chief's craggy face, pushing their way up and over its crown. Then they descended, hurrying out over the vast plains that sprawled eastward toward the Sweet Grass and Bear Paw Mountains. And in their wake they left the mountain appearing serene, highlighted by a sky as blue as the deepest of seas.

We had come to hike the mystical mountain because of its grandeur, unique geology, and intriguing history, little aware that what is normally a jaunt of about ten hours would be extended another sixteen—and by the same cosmic elements that, in part, had lured us to this rugged section of the Rockies.

With the exception of one person, our party was an experienced one. Three of us had spent a week together in tents during the dead of winter, skiing over snow-covered glaciers in Jasper, Alberta. I had climbed Chief Mountain several years prior; two others in the party had climbed Mount Cleveland, Glacier's highest peak (10,466 feet). This park seemed much like our backyard—a place where people go to spend a pleasant day, fully believing they can relax because they are well acquainted with all possible annoyances.

Ascending Chief Mountain is much easier than you might expect. Viewed from the highway, the mountain, with its vertical walls, appears impossible to climb. But several easy, nontechnical climbing routes exist. Perhaps the most intriguing one starts on the Blackfeet Indian Reservation, where you'll need a tribal permit. Begin your climb from a road constructed by the Humble Oil Company. This was the route I had chosen several years ago, and the one we again selected.

After leaving the timber, we came to an immense jumble of rock released by Chief Mountain in 1972. In *A Climber's Guide to Glacier National Park*, J. Gordon Edwards writes, "In August of 1972, thousands of tons of rock fell from Chief Mountain as the entire northeast corner collapsed. The roar was heard as far away as Lake McDonald . . . "

From the jumble of rock we proceeded, as directed by Edwards, toward the westward clump of hills. From there we followed a trail marked by flagging and rock cairns. Then we proceeded upward for a distance of several thousand feet. Near the top we encountered one notch described as Class III, which indicates that it was not a technical pitch.

From the notch the remainder of the climb followed a level course along a narrow ledge. The wind had begun to blow, and for safety we dropped to all fours. Then we proceeded along on rock that carried with it messages of immense passages of time. Embedded there were ripple marks from seas that had once covered flat land. This was Precambrian rock, some of the oldest known to man; 500 million years after its formation, we were scurrying over it.

About five hours after leaving our automobile, we scaled through to the top. Removing our shirts, we enjoyed the hot summer sun and the exhilarating view of our surroundings.

Many climbers, overwhelmed by the view, had hastily attempted to express the emotional impact of it in the mountain's log:

Secretary of War Henry Stimpson climbed Chief Mountain in 1891 and found a bison skull.

"Our quest for a vision fulfilled," wrote a group from California.

"Hurray for the Chief," scribed a seventy-three-year-old man from Montana.

"Grizzlies seen through my binoculars . . . ," wrote another Montana man.

Other climbers noted that it was an Indian who was first lured to the mountain and that he came for his vision quest. This man had come from the area around Flathead Lake, climbed over the high passes, slipped through the territory of the hostile Blackfeet Indians, and climbed up the long slopes to the base of Chief Mountain. Then, knowing others before him had not returned, the warrior dragged himself and a bison skull to the Chief's summit and began fasting.

He remained on the mountain for four nights, using the skull for his pillow, pacing the rocky pinnacle and chanting warrior songs while attempting to make peace with the gods who were to decide his destiny.

The spirit of the mountain attempted to drive the warrior off the peak but, at last, on the fourth night it yielded. The spirit then smoked the peace pipe with the brave and gave him the sacred token, which was to protect him against all peril of battle or of the hunt. He died of old age, the greatest of Flathead warriors. Just before his death he told the young men of the tribe the source of his powerful medicine.

No white man climbed the peak until 1891, when Henry L. Stimpson (secretary of state under President Herbert Hoover and secretary of war under President Franklin Roosevelt) and two friends, one a full-blooded Blackfeet Indian, made the second documented ascent. At the top, Stimpson found the weathered remains of an old bison skull. He left it on the summit where his party found it wedged among the rocks.

In his diary Stimpson noted that weather posed a problem. Almost a century later, we faced the same such forces. North of us, but rapidly moving south toward the Chief, were fast-moving clouds. These were spirits with which we did not wish to contend. It was time to descend.

Near the base of the mountain the storm was beginning to engulf the Chief. Fog had developed, and visibility was soon reduced to about 20 feet. Above us the sky was blue, but below clouds darkened the land. It was colder, too, and rain was beginning to fall. We had walked into a storm that only moments ago had been beneath us. Still, it was only four o'clock in the afternoon, and presumably ample time remained to find the trail.

Four hours later we were still looking for the trail. Compass readings had not helped as no reference points could be seen. The storm now engulfed the entire mountain. In the fog, mud slopes, talus slopes, and fallen rock appeared completely foreign to our four pairs of eyes. Once we found a cairn and thought a trail was nearby. Eagerly we fanned out and began a search, but forty-five minutes later we hadn't located anything that resembled a trail.

An hour before nightfall, we stopped to assess our situation. None of us had any food, but we all had matches and a bit of warm clothing. If we could kindle a fire, we could endure the night. It was time to think in those terms—our Gortex jackets no longer protected us against the steady downpour. One in our party had developed violent chills, and his teeth rattled uncontrollably.

Building a fire was difficult. Wood was waterlogged, even chips derived from whittling sticks to the core were slow to ignite. Shaking our heads, we quickly realized this was not our backyard. Still, the conditions were astounding. This was summer; the first week of August—often the year's hottest time. But these were the mountains—grand, perfectly sublime, and totally unpredictable. How quickly the lessons from other such times had faded.

We smiled grimly as we recalled that weather had attempted to drive the Flathead warrior off the Chief. It seemed appropriate to beseech the spirit of the mountain to set before us a fire-starting kit—and to request a space blanket, more dry clothes, some snacks, and a small tarp. We could be in serious trouble should the rain increase in intensity or we not be able to kindle a fire.

At last we took out the Edwards climbing guide. Its dry pages helped nurture the tiny flame now flickering beneath a jacket spread to prevent rain from snuffing it out. Soon the fire roared.

Night descended, and one in our party jokingly reminded us that only eight hours remained until daylight. We hoped the rain would stop.

Night passed quickly. The fire was warm, and our clothes quickly dried. About 2:00 A.M. the rain changed to snow. We could see our breath mushrooming into the night. The temperature had plummeted. It was colder, much colder, but thankfully the penetrating rain had stopped. The spirit of the mountain had smiled upon us.

At 6:00 A.M. we began our trek out of the timber. The brisk pace warmed our bodies. As we climbed back up the ridge we saw the proper drainage several miles in the distance. Above us the Chief broke through the clouds just once. We hurried on, leaving behind a temperamental edifice, grateful that our more earthly spirits were not mantled by snow.

To Climb the Chief

There are two ways to climb this mountain. One involves a very long day and a round-trip of about 20 miles. The other has you camping overnight at Slide Lake and making the day of your actual climb much shorter. Either way you'll leave from the Lee Creek trailhead, which is about 2 miles from the U.S.–Canadian border.

Drive toward the Chief Mountain Customs, noting when you leave the Blackfeet Indian Reservation and enter Glacier. Drive 2.5 miles from the boundary over the top of a hill to a parking lot on the right-hand side. The trailhead is on the left. Follow the Lee Creek Trail 6.8 miles to Gable Pass. From here either begin the long day climb or continue 1.5 miles to the campground at Slide Lake. Either way the trail from Gable Pass remains the same. The difference is that you are back to your car after one long day or after two not-so-long ones.

From Gable Pass, follow the unofficial trail around Papoose and Ninaki Mountains to the base of Chief Mountain. Usually there are cairns here that you'll follow to the top of Chief. The route to the top is fairly obvious, but if you feel uncomfortable at this point, you might not want to complete the trip. Try again another day.

Mad Wolf Mountain: My Spirit Mound

Along the east front of Glacier National Park, Mad Wolf Mountain rises gently, offering from its flanks and peak unparalleled views of prairie and mountain ranges. The mountain's name recalls a famous Blackfeet Indian orator who camped often in nearby Cut Bank Valley. Mad Wolf was that man, and not far from his tepee the Blackfeet people encountered and killed the Gros Ventre war chief A-koch-kit-ope. Later Mad Wolf described the chief's subsequent transformation to a great bear known as the "Medicine Grizzly."

In summer 2004 I returned to the valley to climb Mad Wolf, the wonderfully rounded dome that looms from the vantage point of the Cut Bank Ranger Station. The climb is one I had put aside for many years, not finding time to climb it even when I worked in the park in the early 1980s as a ranger. As part of my job, I rode the mountain's slopes on my park horse, John, and sometimes encountered black and grizzly bears. In addition to more routine work patrolling backcountry campgrounds, I also rode the slopes of Mad Wolf to prevent trespassing of livestock—my glory days. Here, too, in the mountain's shadow, I reared children; reflected on Glacier's first fatal grizzly bear maulings (and my part in them); peered over land chronicling the infamous "starvation winter"; learned more about Mad Wolf himself; and thrilled to the discovery of an abandoned route to the flanks of a mountain that had come to assume larger-than-life proportions. Now all that remained was to actually climb the mountain.

My climb up Mad Wolf began about a mile south of Cut Bank Ranger Station along a seldom-used trail that once provided access to the long-since-demolished Cut Bank Chalet. I forded Cut Bank Creek, crossing where a bridge once stood—its footings from the late 1940s still discernable. Then I struck out for a now-abandoned trail, which I helped relocate during my days at the ranger station. Despite new vegetation, a familiar tree I once marked along Mad Wolf Creek still stood; nearby was a small path.

The trail spiraled up one of the mountain's flanks, passing through stands of Douglas fir and cow parsnip, the latter a favorite food of grizzlies. Not surprisingly, I saw bear dung all along the trail containing ropes of the large telltale leaves.

Mad Wolf is not the highest of Glacier's mountains, rising only 8,341 feet. Nor is it one that demands technical proficiency. Rather it's a mountain that rewards the hiker with sweeping vistas and skills derived from route-finding. Halfway up and already the mountain was commanding views that on this perfectly clear day stretched more than 100 miles eastward to the many-storied Sweet Grass Hills.

Closer and I could see the trough containing Badger Creek, along which so many Blackfeet Indians starved in 1883. That brutal winter, Almost-a-Dog kept a record of each death by cutting a notch in a willow stick; the number of those marks reached 555. Just the year before, the "tail of the last buffalo" was seen. But land and a species are resilient—as my gaze of now prosperous ranchlands below suggested—and that conclusion gave me hope, a feeling easily reached on a warm July day on Mad Wolf.

From my vantage at this midway point, it would be difficult to ascend the peak. An old trail delineating the park and reservation boundary continued around the east-facing slope, where I soon encountered both cattle and wild horses. When I served as a ranger, it was my job to drive out such animals,

Fireweed frames Mad Wolf, the mountain named for the famous Blackfeet orator, and Bad Marriage.

which competed for food with the once-abundant bighorn sheep. Nightly I would scope the mountainside for wild horses. When the situation required, I would saddle John, ride the slopes, and gallop after the wild horses—having the time of my life—driving the herd back onto the reservation. Now, here on Mad Wolf, the thought struck me that everyone should fashion a spirit mound of his or her own, one that has the power to preserve and recall powerful memories.

Soon I came to a scree slope that wound naturally through a series of steep cliff faces. The route was obvious, and one hour later I reached the summit. The view swept from horizon to horizon. I could see both Medicine Grizzly Peak and Medicine Grizzly Lake. Although the sky was faultlessly blue, strong wind gusts pounded my head. As I sat, I recalled the story Mad Wolf recounted for Walter McClintock in McClintock's book *The Old North Trail.*

As the story went, A-koch-kit-ope (a Gros Ventre medicine man leading tribal members through the mountains east to buffalo grounds on the prairie) was killed by the Blackfeet Indians along the trail that begins near the ranger station, clearly visible in the distance. But A-koch-kit-ope's medicine was such that in death he transformed himself into an enormous grizzly.

Kayaking in Glacier

Kayaking is a relatively new sport to Glacier, but these craft can take you to a number of wonderful areas where few others can go. Such areas include Swiftcurrent Lake to Josephine Lake (with a short portage) on the park's east side at Many Glacier. On the park's west side, there are two great places, both in the North Fork region of the park. One is Bowman Lake, the other is Kintla Lake, and we've chosen a weekend stay at Kintla to show why we as photographers so enjoy this area. Before embarking, you might also want to read our section on rolling a kayak and consider lessons from one of the professional outlets in the Flathead. We've listed two in our appendix.

Kintla Lake, located in the most extreme northwestern portion of Glacier National Park, is probably the most remote lake in the park that can still be accessed by a vehicle. The last 15 miles of the road from Polebridge, however, are bumpy, narrow, and winding. In places you have to check overhead clearance, particularly if you carry kayaks on a roof mount, as do we.

In 1965 while in college, I worked at Kintla as a seasonal ranger and know that days when the lake is perfectly tranquil are rare. But sometimes, in the summer, there are days that are so still, you can almost turn upside down any photos you take of the lake and mountains and not tell the difference.

In the 1960s power boats were allowed, but that's not the case today, which makes it a haven for kayaking—and for photographers. Each morning we arose early, and each morning we tried to improve on the reflection picture of the previous day, realizing, finally, that the human element might add an extra dimension. Positioning, however, had to be precise, and that meant lots of hand signals between Janie and me so as not to disturb other campers still asleep. The results paid off, and Janie's presence added to the images of Starvation Ridge and Starvation Peak (in Canada) and Long Knife Peak (in Montana) reflected in this lake located about 5 miles from the Canadian line.

Since I worked at Kintla, more has been discovered about the area. Indians once used the lake. Because archaeologists found a Folsom point near the campground, digging—even trenches around tents—is not permitted. As well, a 19-foot size restriction has been placed on RVs, not only to create a more wilderness-type atmosphere, but to help protect RV units themselves. We're RVers, but we prefer it this way, and so, when we visit Kintla, we do so with a tent.

For a variety of reasons, Kintla will always be one of our favorite places in the park: certainly because of its beauty, but perhaps as well, because it is ideal for kayaking and it's reasonable to expect to see moose, bears, and foxes along the shores of the lake. And, if you have enough balance to land a fish from a kayak, consider trolling a lure behind.

Some summer days on Kintla Lake are so still, you can turn the photo upside down and not tell the difference.

When you do kayak the lake, be aware that unexpected winds often blow in. We tend to stay close to the north shore, where the trail is located and where a shoreline enables you to land more easily.

Mad Wolf recalled that the next spring, when his people went up the valley to cut lodge poles, a huge grizzly bear swept into camp. Appearing beside the fir tree where the year before the Gros Ventre medicine man had hung his war bonnet, the animal went boldly through camp, eating all the food it found and tearing to pieces hides and parfleches. Afterwards, whenever Mad Wolf's people camped near the fir tree in the canyon, they would see this "Medicine Grizzly." The Blackfeet knew his medicine was strong and were afraid to shoot him.

The story is one I think about often, for grizzly bears have been an integral part of my Montana experience since I first came to Glacier in the 1960s. In 1967, as a ranger stationed in another valley, I encountered an emaciated garbage-fed grizzly that had taken a human life. I thought of that starving bear, and then I thought of the wonderfully healthy bears I had seen in Cut Bank Valley—the "Valley of the Medicine Grizzly."

One June I encountered a grizzly feeding on a dead cow near the ranger station. It bristled and then fled. Another time I rode John along the trail near Pitamakan Pass—also visible from the top of Mad Wolf. On that day the wind was blowing violently and John was nervously swinging his head back and forth. Craning my neck, I saw another bear about 50 feet behind, trailing us. When I reined in, the beast veered and went crashing through the nearby brush and down a steep ravine. Both animals were so enormous that I was certain they were descendents of the Medicine Grizzly.

Perhaps my most exhilarating experience occurred one golden October day several years ago when Janie and I were picnicking along the flanks of Mad Wolf. We'd been talking quietly, but when we looked up we saw two grizzly littermates staring at us. They were 30 to 40 yards away, but reaching us would have been difficult because a deep ravine separated us. From our relatively safe vantage point, we watched as the pair swung their massive paws, excavating huge swaths of dirt in their search for roots and bulbs. They were preparing for hibernation, and as they moved, muscles and fat rippled down the length of their bodies. Finally they stood and stretched to staggering heights before dropping onto all fours to disappear silently into the darkening shadows of late afternoon.

Through the years I've evaluated my many grizzly bear sightings, trying to draw conclusions. The only truly dangerous bear I've ever encountered was the one that fatally mauled a young woman camper in 1967 at Trout Lake, which another ranger, Leonard Landa, and I later killed. The bear had become an aberration possibly because of its advanced age and its habit of feeding on thoughtlessly discarded garbage. (A necropsy revealed that the sow had glass embedded between her molars.)

Grizzly bears are magnificent examples of evolution that sometimes rise to mythological proportions, as in the case of the Medicine Grizzly. Mad Wolf, the man, has also become a mythological figure. Just before he died on May 28, 1902, four large crosses of light appeared about the moon—the sign a great chief is about to die. Turning to his wife, Morning Plume, Mad Wolf whispered words of love and then passed to the Spirit World over the "Wolf Trail" (Milky Way), the path worn across the heavens by the traveling spirits of many generations of the Blackfeet dead.

As I sat there in the late afternoon, looking down on Medicine Grizzly Peak and Lake, I better understood the power and mystery of the land and of the great bears that roam it. A half-moon rose near Medicine Grizzly Peak, plainly visible in the deep blue sky now beginning to darken. Quietly I gathered my belongings and began the long descent down my spirit mound. Although the ranger station no longer waits for me, my tent does, and it is pitched often now at the base of Mad Wolf Mountain.

The trek to Mad Wolf Mountain is about 6 to 7 miles out and back from Cut Bank Ranger Station.

Chapter 5
Glacier Cross-Country Ski Trails

When the interior roads in Glacier National Park are closed to vehicles in winter, they make wonderful cross-country ski trails, as do the low-elevation hiking trails. On the west side of the park, Going-to-the-Sun Road is a popular ski destination. The park is also a great place to snowshoe. First-timers should carry a good map of the park, available at most sporting goods stores in the valley. Access Glacier's great Web site for more information: http://home.nps .gov/applications/glac/ski/xcski.htm.

The following are just a sampling of Glacier's cross-country ski opportunities.

Autumn Creek Loop

When the weather is cooperative, this can be one of the most delightful trips in the park. Along here we've seen groups of ptarmigan comfortably settled in the snow—all puffed up and peering back at us without a touch of fear in their eyes, as though to say, "Any creature out here must be just another ptarmigan."

To facilitate this 6-mile trip, you'll need two vehicles or arrange to have someone transport you the 5 miles to Marias Pass at the completion of your trip.

To reach the trailhead from West Glacier, drive toward East Glacier, past the turnoff to the Izaak Walton Inn, and 5 miles past the Walton Ranger Station to a gated road on your left. Leave one car here and then drive to Marias Pass and park in that parking lot. Transport

Skiing from Marias Pass toward Firebrand Pass, a distance of about 7 miles, is one of the most diverse trips in the park.

your skis across the railroad tracks and scout around a bit to find the Autumn Creek Loop ski trail. Look for orange markers denoting the trail.

Initially the trail passes Three Bears Lake and then, in about a mile, turns south. Throughout the trip you are skiing along the flanks of Elk and Little Dog Mountains, and we've seen ptarmigan in the windswept open areas. The trail is well marked, but when the snow has drifted you may need to pay particular attention to trail markers. The trail is fairly level, but the last 1.5 miles follow a narrow trail. If the snow is crusted, you may generate more speed than you want. Make sure you know how to snowplow—or know how to place the ski poles between your legs and rake the snow with your baskets to create sufficient drag to stop you. On this trip, take your time and look around. The scenery is spectacular.

Lubeck Ranger Station

As an alternative to the Autumn Creek Loop above, you may want to make an even longer trip, traveling from the nearby site of the old Lubeck Ranger Station to East Glacier. Again, you need two cars or someone to transport you.

To find the trailhead, drive on US 2 from Marias Pass toward East Glacier, about 4 miles to the west switch of the Bison Siding. Here you'll take a pull-off that dips down to a parking area. (Here's also where the railroad track changes from doubletrack to singletrack.) The trailhead is on the other side of the track.

Follow the old road (now the trail) 1.4 miles to the trail junction. (A left takes you back toward Marias Pass.) Take the right fork and proceed 1 mile to the next trail junction. If you go left at that junction, you'll be skiing toward Firebrand Pass, 2.4 miles away. Going right takes you to East Glacier, 6.7 miles away. Whichever route you follow, you can't go wrong. We've skied both routes, and this remains one of our favorite winter areas in the park.

Lake McDonald
(5 to 12 miles out and back)

Drive to the head of Lake McDonald and park in the hotel parking lot. From here, during winter, the Going-to-the-Sun Road is unplowed, providing skiers with excursions for as many miles as they can handle. When we've felt particularly energetic, we've skied 5.8 miles one-way to the Avalanche Lake trailhead. Once we continued from the trailhead another 2 miles to the lake itself. In the early 1980s we saw a mountain lion early one morning chasing a herd of elk, although we never learned the outcome.

A more moderate trip from your parked car would be to ski the road 2 miles to the spur road that turns left to the Lake McDonald Ranger Station. At the spur road, ski about 100 yards and cross the bridge. In about another 100 yards, look for a trail on your right that parallels McDonald Creek. This trail is about

A ptarmigan in winter plumage blends with its surroundings, in insulating snow where it's warm and snug.

1 mile long and affords wonderful views of the river crusted over with ice. In about a mile the trail comes to a right turn; you'll see a bridge that crosses McDonald Creek. Cross it, link up again with the road, and then continue along the road, keeping abreast of Sacred Dancing Cascade, which you first encountered at the bridge. From the bridge you have about 3 miles before arriving at your car. Any additional skiing you do along the road increases your mileage—and your day afield.

McGee Meadow Loop
(12-mile loop)

From the West Glacier entrance, proceed to the T intersection and turn left. Drive 1 mile (passing the turnoff to Apgar Village) and park at the winter gate located at the foot of Camas Road. Ski 5 miles, always uphill, to the Camas Creek overlook. Ski east across the meadow (there's a trail, but it's not always easy to find). Maintain this direction until you come to what in summer is a dirt road, officially known as the Inside North Fork Road. Ski south (right) on this road downhill, passing in 4 miles the turn to the Fish Creek Campground. Continue on this unplowed road, following the signs to Apgar, for 2 miles back to your car. For a less strenuous trip, reverse the above directions.

Will Friedner pauses along McDonald Creek, just below Sacred Dancing Cascade, a delightful and easy trip.

Bowman Lake

From Columbia Falls pick up the North Fork Road. Follow it (paralleling the ice-covered North Fork River much of the way) 30 miles to the Polebridge Mercantile. Stop in and say hello to the owners, buy some of their cookies, and then drive 2 more miles to the Polebridge Ranger Station. From Polebridge follow the well-marked unplowed road 6 miles to Bowman Lake. The trail passes through areas burned by the fires of the late 1990s and early 2000s. Even buried with snow, the woods show the dramatic recovery nature makes following a fire. Look for moose, elk, deer, and owls and other birds of prey.

Old Flathead Ranger Station
(5 miles one-way)

From the West entrance, drive 0.5 mile to the first turn on your left. Follow this road 0.5 mile to the T junction and turn right. On your left in 0.25 mile you'll come to a winter gate; park your car here. Start by skiing to the Quarter Circle Bridge. Cross the bridge and continue your ski 0.75 mile to a road junction. A right turn takes you to Apgar Lookout—another, albeit *very* rugged, option. Turn left and ski across hill and dale, stream and bridge, to the old Flathead Ranger Station. The station is no longer manned but serves as mute testimony to the isolated lives led by some of the park's early-day rangers.

The park produces an excellent brochure for these and other skiing and snowshoe trails. Or go online for more information: http://home.nps.gov/applications/glac/ski/xcski.htm.

Winter snows pile up, cut only by the power of Grinnell Creek in Many Glacier Valley, seen following a 6-mile ski trip.

Chapter 6
Black Bears and Grizzlies

When comparing the various traits of grizzly and black bears, there is one distinct feature that immediately separates the two species—temperament. Where one is inclined to be docile, the other is aggressive. Where one usually retreats, the other advances. The reason for this behavior is linked to environmental features that existed long ago.

According to paleontologists, based on fossil remains, grizzly bears first came on the scene about one million years ago. *Ursus americanus*, the more docile black bear, preceded the grizzly by another million years. Both animals, however, evolved from a common ancestral species, *Ursus etruscus*, with subsequent environmental factors shaping the two distinct personalities.

U. etruscus lived in Asia, where it was essentially an inhabitant of the forest. But climatic changes caused trees to disappear. As the forest became sparse, the bears of the resultant tundra adapted. To cope with the lack of cover, *U. etruscus* had to develop a new disposition. No longer could it retreat from danger by taking to the trees; no longer could it protect its offspring by sending them into high branches. Instead, to survive attacks from other predators, the evolving grizzly had to become more powerful. On the treeless prairie, sows were forced to defend their cubs aggressively. Assisting her were such adaptations as long claws (useless for climbing trees) and a large physical stature. Huge back muscles evolved for digging up sod in search of underground-dwelling rodents and the roots, tubers, and bulbs of plants associated with the plains. These back muscles appear as the prominent shoulder hump of the grizzly.

These adaptive characteristics enabled the sow to defend herself and her cubs against any potential foe. Where black bear sows retreated, *Ursus arctos*,

Glacier National Park is home to about 300 grizzly bears. We met up with this one in Many Glacier Valley, along the trail to Iceberg Lake.

What Kind of Bear Is That?

Grizzly Bear

- Blond to nearly black, sometimes with silver-tipped guard hairs that give a "grizzled" appearance
- Concave or dished-in face
- Large hump of heavy muscle above the shoulders
- Light-colored claws 1.5–4 inches long
- 3–4 feet tall at the shoulder, often more than 6–8 feet when standing
- Weighs 200–700 pounds

Black Bear

- Black, brown, cinnamon, or blond with a lighter-colored muzzle
- Straighter facial profile than the grizzly's from nose to ears
- Dark-colored claws up to 1.5 inches long
- 2–4 feet tall at the shoulder and stands up to 4–5 feet
- Weighs 150–500 pounds
- Relatively smaller head than the grizzly

the evolved grizzly, advanced, and this characteristic was firmly imprinted on the cubs. Not surprisingly, many grizzly bear attacks today involve mothers with their cubs.

These evolutionary changes took place in Asia. Later, as the bridge connecting North America and Asia began to grow, *U. arctos* crossed over to greet the black bear, its predecessor by almost 250,000 years. About the same time, the grizzly had its first recorded encounters with man—and some of those occurred in Glacier National Park. Some of the earliest encounters involved Native Americans, as the treatise on my climb up Mad Wolf suggests.

Park visitors continue to encounter grizzlies today, and park records indicate that sightings are made almost daily during the summer. It's fortunate, but incredible that more injuries don't occur. Today park managers do a pretty good job of separating man and bear. But in the park's early days, man-bear contact was condoned. Two fatal maulings in 1967—in the course of a single evening!—changed all that.

Past misfortunes often resulted from visitors' complete lack of appreciation of the wild nature of animals. For example, parents used food to lure bears into their cars so they might photograph the animals next to their children. Here are a few more examples extracted from the old records:

1939: 3 persons injured when they fed bears; 3 others injured while watching the feeding; 1 injury when visitor stepped between sow and cub . . .

1941: Lone unknown bear climbed on running board, pulled windshield and broke it . . .

1947: 4 personal injuries to visitor while feeding bears of unknown species . . .

1948: 2 people injured by black bears while feeding them chocolates. Woman scratched below eye; man scratched on lip . . .

1958: While walking with dog, [a man was attacked by a] lone GB . . .

Even before 1967, the park understood the potential danger and recognized some contributing factors of its own, like the incredible buildup of garbage. I was working in Glacier as a seasonal ranger in 1967 and once helped the chief ranger bag up and load into a helicopter seventeen burlap sacks of garbage from the Trout Lake area. Garbage, as I reported for a major story in *Smithsonian* magazine, had contributed directly to the park's first two fatal maulings, one at Granite Park Chalet, the other at Trout Lake. Both occurred the same night in 1967.

Following those twin tragedies, the park created a comprehensive Bear Management Plan, spelling out the ways in which people should conduct themselves when in bear country. In addition, you can be assured that garbage is

Black bears now number between 600 and 700 in Glacier National Park and are seen frequently along Fish Creek Road; do not disturb them.

gone from all backcountry campsites and that park managers are very much on top of things. People caught feeding bears are immediately cited, and dogs are no longer allowed on backcountry trails in the park, and there's a very good reason for the rule. If a dog is loose and encounters a bear, it will return to its owner for protection.

Now, if you see a bear, generally it will be under completely natural conditions, and most likely, it will run. For all these reasons, we both feel safer sleeping on the ground in a tent than we do combating traffic on our way to the park.

Tips on Finding Bears

The park contains approximately 600 black bears and about 300 grizzly bears. (Ongoing DNA studies will determine more exact populations.) If you're hiking a backcountry trail, you'll want to see bears, but you'll want to see them first—and from a safe distance. High-country meadows are always good places to see grizzlies, but they often blend with the landscape, so take along a pair of binoculars. In spring grizzlies seek out the roots of glacier lily bulbs, and the trail to Hidden Lake is loaded with them. Stay on the boardwalk and scan the meadows.

One of the best places to see bears routinely is the Many Glacier Valley. Park in the Swiftcurrent Motor Inn parking lot and then scan the hillside behind the lodge with binoculars or, even better, with a spotting scope. Most people who spend time here find grizzlies.

Be Cautious around Wildlife

Black bears, grizzlies, and mountain lions inhabit northwest Montana. Be aware that you could encounter one of these animals, though it is unlikely. There are a few simple precautions you should take, and always remember that along with the thrill of seeing animals in their native setting, it is your obligation to behave in a responsible manner.

The first thing you should do is read all relevant information and guidelines if you plan to hike or camp in bear country. Glacier National Park has tons of information and many short films you can view that cover potentially dangerous wildlife.

In bear country, stay alert and make noise, especially when approaching blind corners on a hike. If you carry bear bells, be aware that their sound really doesn't carry very far. Carry pepper spray (a can for each person), know how to use it, and keep it accessible—not buried in your pack.

If you encounter any wildlife, do not approach closely for photos or any other reason. Even the mountain sheep and goats need their space and can be dangerous when pushed.

If you should surprise a grizzly bear, stay quiet and back away slowly, avoiding direct eye contact. Try to get off the bear's trail. Stop immediately if your movements are upsetting the bear. Signs of bear agitation include a swaying head, clacking teeth, a lowered head, and laid-back ears. Never run or yell. Keep your pack on.

In case of an attack, drop to the ground on your stomach or assume a fetal position. Cover the back of your neck with your hands. Do not move until you are sure the bear has really left the vicinity.

Ranger Bill Hutchison demonstrates the proper use of bear spray.

Most negative bear encounters happen when a bear is surprised, when people run into a sow with cubs, and when food isn't stored properly. In the backcountry you need to hang your food or use a bear-resistant box.

If you encounter a black bear or a mountain lion, yell, throw things, and generally act aggressively, but do not run away. If attacked, fight the animal off if possible. It is believed that hikers traveling in groups generally are less prone to being attacked by bears. The park gives advice for surprise encounters and predatory attacks.

Finally, remember that any species of wild animal poses a potential threat—especially females with their young.

Section II:
The Flathead Valley

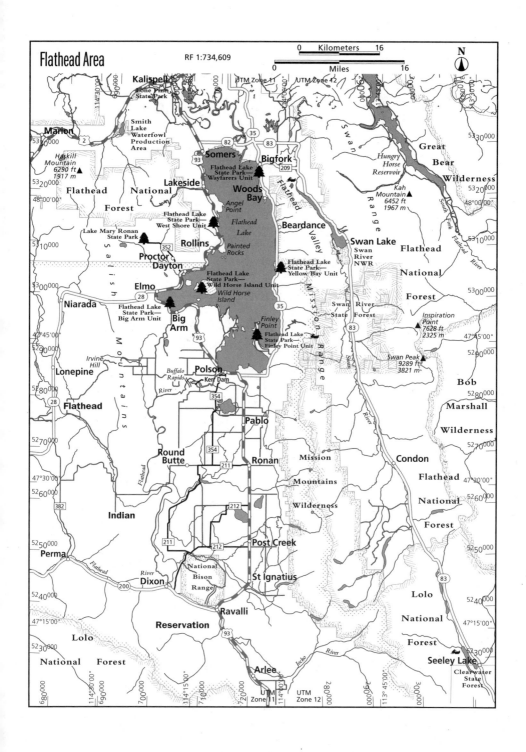

Flathead Area

RF 1:734,609

Kilometers

0   16

0   16

Miles

N

Kalispell
Lone Pine State Park

UTM Zone 11   UTM Zone 12

Marion

Smith Lake Waterfowl Production Area

Haskill Mountain 6290 ft 1917 m

Somers
Bigfork

Flathead Lake State Park— Wayfarers Unit

Woods Bay

Hungry Horse Reservoir

Great Bear Wilderness

Flathead National Forest

Lakeside

Kah Mountain 6452 ft 1967 m

Angel Point

Flathead Lake

Beardance

Lake Mary Ronan State Park

Flathead Lake State Park— West Shore Unit

Rollins

Painted Rocks

Swan Lake
Swan River NWR

Flathead

Proctor
Dayton

Flathead Lake State Park— Yellow Bay Unit

National

Elmo

Flathead Lake State Park— Wild Horse Island Unit

Wild Horse Island

Forest

Niarada

Flathead Lake State Park— Big Arm Unit

Big Arm

Finley Point

Flathead Lake State Park— Finley Point Unit

Inspiration Point 7628 ft 2325 m

Lonepine

Irvine Hill

Buffalo Rapids

River

Polson

Kerr Dam

Swan River State Forest

Swan Peak 9289 ft 3821 m

Bob

Flathead

Round Butte

Pablo

Ronan

Mission

Marshall

Condon

Wilderness

Indian

Mountains

Wilderness

Flathead

National

Forest

Perma

Post Creek

Dixon

National Bison Range

St Ignatius

Lolo

Ravalli

Reservation

National

Lolo

Forest

National   Forest

Seeley Lake

Clearwater State Forest

Arlee

UTM Zone 11   UTM Zone 12

Chapter 7
A Room with a View

When I first saw Flathead Lake forty years ago, I gazed at the immensity of the waters and the beauty of the mountains and tried to contain myself. As a teenager, my heart raced and my mind soared. Why, I could launch a canoe near Glacier National Park and a week later reach Flathead Lake. From there I could continue for yet another week to the lake's end, make a small portage, and still keep right on going.

Today my résumé from the outdoors includes some of those trips and certainly will again. But today I don't always like to sleep on the ground or go for extended periods without a shower. Flathead Lake Country has within its expanses an abundance of places to camp, providing proximity to less intense but still exciting adventures. And so we set out on a two-week trip to refamiliarize ourselves with our backyard. During our explorations we toured museums and art galleries and attended plays. But we also pitted ourselves against nature in ways that almost rivaled the thrilling outings of my youth in a place that has—as Janie likes to say—"a room with a view."

Most recently we began an exploration of Flathead's Lake Country by pulling into Wayfarers State Park, located just outside Bigfork. The campground is one of five located around the lake managed under the auspices of Montana Fish, Wildlife and Parks (FWP). The next day we toured Bigfork, with its award-winning summer playhouse, numerous art galleries, and fine dining.

Bigfork is also a jumping-off spot for the Jewel Basin Hiking Area, a spectacular sweep of more than 15,000 wilderness acres managed exclusively for hikers. Hikes there are popular, say the campground host and hostess at Wayfarer, because they provide perspectives on Flathead Lake—and because they are relatively easy.

Much of the elevation gain can be accomplished by car. Following a forty-five-minute drive up the steep and sometime rutted road, we arrived at the Jewel Basin parking lot—elevation 6,437 feet. From there several trails radiate out. We chose one that would take us to the top of Mount Aeneas.

At 7,528 feet, Aeneas is the highest peak in the Swan Mountains. A gradual 3-mile trail provides sweeping views of Flathead Lake and its surroundings. In the distant north we could see Glacier National Park; to our west and east were endless ranges of mountains with names like Salish, Columbia, and Mission. From several vantage points we could also see Wild Horse, the largest of the

Osprey, which are numerous in the region, have a commanding view over the Flathead Valley.

lake's islands and one to which we wanted to kayak. But most significantly, we could better appreciate the immensity of the lake as it stretched from Somers and Bigfork south to Polson.

At 27 miles long and 15 miles wide at its widest point, Flathead is the largest freshwater lake west of the Mississippi River. Not surprisingly, the lake claims some of the state's best fishing, something on which a number of Flathead Lake guides have capitalized.

In addition to the state park campgrounds such as Wayfarers, about fifteen other campgrounds rim the lake. To reach these sites, you drive past trees and telephone poles on top of which ospreys have built their nests. You drive through small lake villages where skiffs, dories, sailboats, and old barges bob on the water.

We drove along the lake's east side, passing through quiet coves like Yellow Bay and Polson, with its eclectic marina. We were bound for a campground just outside Polson owned and operated by friends who had made their KOA into an award-winning site.

From there we made a day trip to the National Bison Range just 25 miles to the south. It's a tour no one who loves wildlife should miss, particularly during the July and August mating season, when huge bull bison collide.

We also toured a number of museums and went for a late-evening cruise on the *Far West*, a boat that sometimes features the Montana Lite Jazz Band. Combine the seductive beat of "Moon Glow" with a meal from the *Far West*, set those ingredients against the evening glow of reds and oranges shifting on soft waters, and life is very, very good.

Flathead Lake provides a backdrop for several museums. Central School Museum in Kalispell, a town just north of the lake, presents a thoughtful array of artifacts. Some offer insights about the first steamers to ply the lake and river systems—and the logging communities upon which those steamers depended.

Miracle of America Museum near Polson is owned by Gil Mangels, who has long had a passion for patriotism and for American history. His vast display includes military memorabilia and items from the homestead era.

Just south of Ronan, the Nine Pipes Museum serves as a testimony to Bud and Laurel Cheff's vision for the area's human and natural history. Thirty years ago, Bud found a war club dating back 150 years inside an old cave along a bank of the Flathead River. "That set the stage," said Cheff. "I wanted to know why a man might have stayed here. Was he simply seeking shelter from the elements? Was he trying to escape enemies, and, if so, was he successful?"

Perhaps one of the most interesting items in their collection is a brain-tanned deer hide containing a series of hand-drawn pictures. According to Cheff, the hide contains stories referred to by Native Americans as their "Winter Count." The hide represents a time when members of a particular tribe gathered in winter to collect the most significant events of the year and record their essence on an animal hide.

Big Arm State Campground, just 20 miles north of Polson along the lake's western shore, is a great place for kayakers because of its proximity to Wild Horse Island.

Jazz musician Jim Andler often plays on the Far West *summer cruise boat, which departs from Lakeside.*

Legend has it that Wild Horse Island derived its name from the Kootenai Indians' practice of driving their horses into the glacial waters of Flathead Lake and then swimming them to the island. But the 2,156-acre island provided such a secure hiding place for the half-tamed horses that many were overlooked. Those animals soon reverted to their natural state, giving the island its name.

On a windless day, the several-mile kayak trip to the island takes an hour, and it was this trip that stirred dreams from my youth. If you have access to a kayak and the day promises to be calm, I recommend making the trip. If you prefer, you can rent a powerboat at Polson, join a Wild Horse charter cruise, or join a kayak group led by an expert. (See Appendix A for listings of lake charter cruises and kayak companies.)

Our destination was Skeeko Bay. As we beached our crafts, we saw a small herd of bighorn sheep. But everyone wonders if the island still has wild horses. We knew it did and were determined to find and photograph them.

We began our search for horses and other wildlife by following a trail that led a short distance from the shore to an old homestead cabin. From the cabin the trail climbed about 700 feet. Here and there we saw signs of horses but no trace of the horses themselves. We continued our climb, wandering among fields of flowers, extensive grasslands, ponderosa pines, and Douglas fir. As we hiked we saw huge deer. Because hunting is not permitted on Wild Horse, wildlife here has become somewhat tolerant of humans.

The day was warm as we sauntered along. A breeze blew down the slope, and it was then that we found our wild horses in a small ravine. They were not unduly alarmed, and for a moment—*click, click*—they stood erect as though posing for our cameras. They moved, however, when several deer crossed between them and us. Then they went galloping off, angling toward the highest hill. Although we followed, we never saw the horses again.

An hour later we reached the top, and from this vantage point we again came to appreciate just how huge this corner of the world is that contains Flathead Lake. Days earlier we had been on top of Mount Aeneas, and even though it must have been 30 miles in the distance—and sometimes veiled in clouds— we could see the commanding peak. Here on Wild Horse, there was something about the juxtaposition of water and land that added wonder to all our activities. Here our accomplishments seemed surreal—the substance of far-fetched youthful dreams, reminding me of when I first set eyes on the Flathead.

Our room with its view also made us grateful for the technological ease that enables people to better enjoy beauty and place at any time in life. As we pushed our kayaks off from Wild Horse Island, we were anxious for a hot shower and a soft bed—but anxious, too, to further reacquaint ourselves with the many aspects of the Flathead that remain for us such an irresistible force.

Rolling a Kayak—It's All Counterintuitive

Lesson One: It's not normal to hang upside down in a kayak—trying to gain a perch for placement of your paddle on the water's surface so that you can then right yourself with a flick of the hip, but it's what I found myself doing in the spring of 2006.

Kayaking has become one of our obsessions here in the Flathead Valley, because there are so many incredible places to go in both Glacier and the Flathead. But to enjoy the sport to its fullest, I thought it might be beneficial to learn everything possible about the sport. I'm no spring chicken, so it's my thought that if I can do it, so can anyone who puts their mind to it. But after one lesson, I'm not there yet, and I liken my lack of complete success in the first lesson to that of a child trying to pat his head while rubbing his stomach for the first time. I suspect if I hadn't learned that maneuver as a child, learning it now might be a bit more difficult.

Essentially what you're trying to do is bring your paddle to the water's surface and then sweep it as you simultaneously flick your hip, all while upside down. "It's not a power thing," repeated Sue Conrad of Silver Moon Kayak Company. "It's a coordination thing. You've got to put together the independent actions of hip flick with paddle sweep." Between gulps of air and the clearing of my Eustachian tubes, I also recall Sue saying that it's a confidence thing, too, for you've got to get used to hanging upside down and then believing—as you hold your breath—that you'll be righted before you run out of oxygen.

Sue said I did well, but I know some have grasped the procedure with one lesson, though others struggle throughout an entire season...

Bert Gildart practices the hip flick with paddle sweep on Flathead Lake.

Lesson Two: Bottom line, I guess, is that I made one successful roll during my second lesson. But I had believed that after I rolled the kayak—once—I'd then be able to perform the roll with grace and precision henceforth and forevermore.

Wrong!

A modicum of success does not confer talent. Excellence in rolling a kayak derives from much continued practice. There is so much that goes into a successful roll that although you might luck out—once—fine-tuning the skill requires dedication. But one roll is a start, and after watching a training video dozens of times, I understand the concepts. My target's in sight.

The proper roll starts with the "set up," a position in which you lean hard into the side of the kayak at an angle of about 10 o'clock to your craft's long axis. This is when it becomes counterintuitive: Now you dump—on purpose. Then, from an upside-down position you check that the shaft of your paddle is parallel to the side of the kayak and slightly above the water's surface. And here's where it gets really tough.

In theory, you are supposed to sweep the surface of the water, blade angled in such a way that it doesn't dig into the water. If your blade is mis-angled the slightest bit, it will dig down hard, and as Sue says, "It will throw you out of your roll."

I know exactly what she's saying as I am a textbook example of falling out of the roll.

At the same time you are skimming the surface of the water with your blade, you are supposed to be executing that hip flip, and if done properly, the entire action is smooth and graceful. That, I can see is going to take practice. Nevertheless, I lack total confidence and ask for yet another lesson. Sue believes that might be beneficial, but then spoke words that were music to my ears. "After that," she laughed, "I'm gonna have to wean you from your instructor. I think you're about ready to face the world alone."

As I've said to others, "If I can do it, I suspect anyone determined to do so can also do it." Just find yourself a good instructor, and then be ready to spend lots of time practicing. But think of the rewards of being able to look the world in the eye and say, "I can roll a kayak."

Chapter 8
What Makes the Valley
Exploring Towns of the Past

The Flathead Valley contains a number of towns—each worthy of exploration. Should you want to visit the towns in one fell swoop, we suggest that you grab a map and this guide. Plan on a several-day trip, staying in motels or camping as you go at one of the valley's forty-some campgrounds. Along the way you'll find museums galore—and lots of helpful people. For perspective, we'll start with a bit of history.

Although Lewis and Clark have gotten all the credit, David Thompson was perhaps the first white man to see the Flathead Valley. Thompson was sent here in 1808 by his employers (Canada's North West Company) to explore the area and establish trade with the Indians. Coming from Calgary, Canada, he and his party descended the Kootenai River into Montana, where Thompson's lieutenant established the first trading post in what is now the town of Libby.

In 1809 Thompson ranged far and wide through Flathead country, trading beads, jewelry, tobacco, and other merchandise for fur pelts. His fair dealings so impressed the Indians that they offered friendship as well as trades. Thompson first learned of Flathead Lake—called the Salish by the Indians—on March 1, 1809. He described the lake as being 4 to 5 miles by 20, but he obviously had actually seen only Polson Bay, with much of the lake hidden behind islands.

Thompson left this region in 1812, but his trusted lieutenant, Jocko Finley, remained, setting up trading posts. Finley Point, on the lake northeast of Polson, was named for Finley's grandson, Piol. Many of Finley's descendents still live here, and a river, a mountain range, and a valley carry the name of Jocko.

Angus McDonald, a Scot, also contributed greatly to white settlement and development here. He came to America in 1838 with the Hudson's Bay Company and, like David Thompson, soon became well known as a fair and trusted man. He married an Indian woman and took part in native life.

In 1846–67 McDonald and Neil McArthur constructed Fort Connah (*conenaw*), located about 6 miles north of St. Ignatius. The fort dealt mostly in buffalo goods from the Indians, giving trade goods in return. McDonald was in charge of the fort for nineteen years, after which his son, Duncan, took over. The last operating fur post in the territory, Fort Connah was forced by economic reasons to close in 1871. Today only one of the original buildings, a small log cabin, still stands.

McDonald finally retired to the Mission Valley, living and ranching at the Fort Connah site until he died in 1889. His name lives on. Looming 10,000 feet over Ronan, McDonald's Peak overlooks the fort's remains. A small lake reposes at its base, and upslope is a glacier that also bears his name. Lake McDonald in Glacier National Park became a tribute to the family, who still prize the bagpipes McDonald brought from Scotland.

Early Transportation

The lack of roads in the mountainous terrain made early transportation in the Flathead Valley difficult. Before 1885 all traffic was by wagon. To reach the country north of Flathead Lake in 1887, travelers and settlers took the Northern Pacific Railroad spur to Ravalli, Montana. They then went by wagon or stage as far north as the south shore of Flathead Lake. In 1888 Charles Allard Sr. started a mail and passenger stage line from Ravalli to what is now the town of Polson. Passing around Flathead Lake still was difficult, but many attempted the trip, either from necessity or lured by the beauty of what lie ahead.

For a quarter century, starting in 1885, steamboats chugged on the lake from the Flathead River at Demersville (a few miles south of present-day Kalispell) down to the docks at Polson and back again. When this proved successful, more steamers were built, some designed as tugs, others as barges. One of the last ships built on the lake was the *Helena*, built by James Kehoe, whose family still resides in the area. In 1924 the *Helena* ran into the most severe storm ever recorded on Flathead Lake, somehow managing to get to safety. The last boat to serve communities on the lake, the *Helena* was dismantled in 1932. With the completion of the highway on the west shore of the lake in the 1930s, there was no longer a need for the steamboats chugging through Montana's largest natural lake.

River Towns

Columbia Falls

The first settlers arrived in Columbia Falls in 1890; among these were Mickey Berne ("Uncle Mickey") and his brother, Billy. Consulting with Frank Langford of the Great Northern Railroad, the idea was to develop a town site that would be a division point for the Great Northern Railroad. When the deal didn't work out, the division point was located first in Kalispell and then in Whitefish.

Langford still wanted his town site. To obtain it, he "fetched" an Indian woman, Emma Laframboise. The law provided that an Indian could claim 170 acres of land in these parts, and acquisition of land by Emma took less time than the homesteading process. The town site company subsequently bought her out, but the name of Emma Laframboise is on every property abstract in the original part of Columbia Falls. In its earliest years, the town had a brickyard, twenty-one saloons, and a post office called Monaco. On July 1, 1891, the name was changed to Columbia, as fitting for a new community near the headwaters of the Columbia River. When the name Columbia was denied by the U.S. Postal Service, the word "Falls" was added, even though no falls exist in the town.

The town struggled economically until after World War II, when it experienced a grand economic comeback. The lumber industry took off and the 564-foot-high concrete Hungry Horse Dam and Anaconda's aluminum-reduction works were constructed. Today Plum Creek Timber and Columbia Falls Aluminum are the dominant employers. Columbia Falls also enjoys the nickname of "Gateway to Glacier."

Kalispell

Kalispell is the largest city in the Flathead Valley. Since 2000 its population has grown almost 10 percent, prompting record real-estate sales and development as well as a retail boom. Several early towns preceded Kalispell in the same vicinity. Ashley, a mile west of the current city's business section, has been called the first real town in the Flathead Valley, with a post office established in 1884. Demersville, founded in 1887, lasted only a few short years.

The first residents of present-day Kalispell were the Kalispell or Pend d'Oreille Indians. The earliest visitors called the landmarks Kalispell River, Kalispell Valley, and Kalispell Lake, for the Indian tribe dwelling in the area. The Salish people (or Flathead Indians) are a large group related to the more northern (northern Idaho) Pend d'Oreille.

Hudson's Bay Company trader Joseph Howse built a post near present-day Kalispell in 1810, which lasted only one trading season. Eight decades would pass before a permanent settlement was established.

Charles E. Conrad is recognized as Kalispell's founding father. He and his brother came to the Montana Territory in 1868 on a steamboat, first settling in Fort Benton on the Missouri River. Conrad soon had a thriving freight business going and became one of the territory's wealthiest men. On the advice of Jim Hill, an old friend and the main force behind the Great Northern Railroad, Conrad moved to the Flathead and formed the Kalispell Townsite Company. Conrad kept seventy-two acres on which he built a twenty-three-room Norman-style home, a stable complex, and a forty-three-acre hunting preserve. The now-restored Conrad Mansion, donated to the City of Kalispell in 1975, is a lovely visitor attraction, easily identified by the beautiful stone walls surrounding it. The entire 300 block east contains the mansion, which is bordered by Woodland Avenue in the front and Sixth Avenue East in the rear. For information call (406) 755-2166.

By the time the town was incorporated in April 1892, Kalispell had twenty-three saloons, several gambling establishments and dance halls, two Chinese restaurants, two Chinese laundries, and four general stores. Rhythmic chanting and drum beating by the Indians reverberated through town on many evenings.

Agriculture, forest products, and tourism remain the mainstay of the economy of the Flathead Valley. Sweet cherries, Christmas trees, grain, alfalfa, seed potatoes, honey, dairy products, and cattle are the main crops produced by area farmers and ranchers. Manufacturing firms produce concrete, fiberglass products, semiconductor equipment, log and wood homes, and plastic molding.

Whitefish

Well into the late 1800s, the north end of the Flathead remained wilderness. The forest was dense, and the lakes were deep and blue. One by one, choice locations were discovered and homesteaded. John Morton was one of the first to settle near Whitefish Lake, carving a living from the wilderness by ranching and logging.

At its beginning, Whitefish was defined by logging and then the railroad, which arrived in 1902, bringing even more employment. At the time, loggers, who floated thousands of logs downriver to the mill at Somers, were not too concerned with appearances. They left thousands of stumps in and around the new town, eventually leading to the nickname "Stumptown." About 1910, "Weary Willies"—"guests" of the city jail—were put to work clearing the town of stumps. "If they refuse to work," said the city marshal, "put them in jail on a bread-and-water diet."

Whitefish was named for the lake, which, in turn, was named for the abundant whitefish the lake contained. The 1905 census recorded 950 inhabitants.

Whitefish Lake State Park

Located on Dog Bay on beautiful Whitefish Lake, Whitefish Lake State Park offers camping year-round. The mountain views, fishing, and boating are great on this lake. Don't forget to purchase a Montana fishing license, or you'll be jealous of what you see the anglers bringing in!

In the winter, vault toilets are available, but no water; fees are $12 per day during this time. In-season fees are $15 per day, with a seven-day stay limit. The park sits beside an active railroad track; however, it is also right next to the golf course and offers a new boat ramp.

To reach the park, take U.S. Highway 93 north from Kalispell to Whitefish. Once in Whitefish, follow signs for US 93 West, toward the town of Eureka. Go about 3 miles to State Park Road on your right and follow it to the park.

Call (406) 862-3991 for more information, or call the Parks Department in Kalispell (406) 752-5501.

As early as 1935, skiers had schussed down the slopes north of town. The Whitefish Hell-Roaring Ski Club was organized, and in 1947 Winter Sports, Inc., formed and began operating "The Big Mountain." Since then a thoroughly modern ski resort has evolved, with the annual Whitefish Winter Carnival making its first appearance in 1960. Today the town—with its eclectic stores and proximity to Whitefish Lake, Big Mountain, and Glacier National Park—is internationally recognized as a premier vacation spot.

In 2005 Whitefish celebrated the one-hundredth anniversary of its incorporation by placing a time capsule containing about forty artifacts in a historic building.

Lake Towns

Lake towns as well as individual dwellings have been established along the shoreline of Flathead Lake. Polson, at the south end (on U.S. Highway 93) was the site of the first settlement on the lake's banks.

Polson

Around 1840 a French-Canadian named Abraham Finley explored the area with one of Father DeSmet's parties. Finley liked the area and began operating a ferry across the lower Flathead River at the site of present-day Polson. In 1869 Baptiste Aeneas bought the ferry from Finley and built a log cabin, the first residence in Polson. In 1884 David Polson, a talented violinist, arrived from Connecticut; he attracted other musicians. Polson played his music and raised horses and cattle. The town grew enough to warrant a name, and the townsfolk selected David Polson and Baptiste Aeneas to choose it. They settled on Polson, and the town was incorporated in 1910 with a population of 600. The Polson Bridge was soon built to provide a better river crossing.

Settlement progressed north along the west shore of the lake. The west shore wagon trail provided the first means of transportation into the upper Flathead area. In his book *Flathead Lake, From Glaciers to Cherries*, R. C. Robbin talks about that rough wagon road, relating the story of the McCarthy family.

"It was a road in name only. No grading had been done, no rocks removed from it, and the stumps were so high that the wagon axles would barely pass over them. Our wagon mired in mud . . . Mr. McCarthy walked ahead to scout the road. South of present-day Lakeside the caravan came to a steep hill. . . . Parts of the goods in each wagon had to be unloaded. . . . The hill crossing took several days. . . . Old Mr. McCarthy referred to this hill as 'Angel Hill' because it was 'so high that the angels roosted on it.'"

The name still stands.

Today Polson is a still-growing ranch and tourist community, billing itself as the "Port City on Fabulous Flathead Lake." It boasts of fishing, sailing, boat

Bigfork Harbor is encircled by snow.

touring, rafting, rodeos, powwows, golf courses, many fine campgrounds, and room to breathe and grow.

Elmo, Big Arm, Dayton, and Rollins

Between Angel Hill and Polson lie Elmo and Big Arm. Elmo was apparently named for a Kootenai Indian. Today the town is home to many Kootenai.

Big Arm is characterized by its resorts, which allow access to Big Arm Bay. North of Big Arm lies Dayton, a farming community wrapped around its own little bay. Its post office opened in 1893, making it one of the oldest settlements on the west shore.

Rollins, named for Thenault Rollins in 1904, is an intriguing community. Rollins Landing was busy from about 1895 through the 1930s. In addition, the Dewey Lumber Company of Polson kept a big dock at Rollins for its timber activities. You'll see open meadows and bluffs, a corner store, a post office, and a grocery, but the residents of Rollins are mostly out of sight, nestled in pockets around Sessions Point, and Crescent and Dewey's Bays.

Lakeside

The next town north on the west shore is Lakeside. In 1901 John Stoner opened the first post office there, naming it Chautauqua for a popular cultural and religious movement founded at Lake Chautauqua, New York, in 1874.

Chautauqua became a kind of generic name for similar efforts to promote education and enlightened understanding at a time when schooling was not always available to everyone who wanted it. In 1896 a group of Epworth Methodist Church Congregationalists sought to create a facsimile Chautauqua site on the Flathead lakeshore. The Reverend W. W. Van Orsdel, known as "Brother Van," helped acquire some 240 acres of prime lakeshore property at present-day Lakeside. Continuing efforts to launch Chautauqua failed, and by 1900 the dream had ended and the lands had been disposed of. Today Lakeside is a busy lakefront resort town of restaurants, motels, campgrounds, and boats, to mention just a few offerings. The inception of Blacktail Mountain Ski Resort in 1998 also bolstered the town's economy.

Somers

At the extreme northwest tip of Flathead Lake is the rural town of Somers, once the valley's second largest community. Founded in 1901 as a mill town for the John O'Brien Lumber Company, the town was named for George Somers, an official with the Great Northern Railroad, for which the town provided ties and timbers.

The major port on the northern end of Flathead Lake, Somers served as headquarters for some of the valley's ambitious logging operations and as a terminus for passengers and freight making connections between the Great Northern Railroad to the north and the Northern Pacific Railroad to the south.

Somers became the Somers Lumber Company town and existed as such until 1948, when the vast mill closed. Today only a forest of weathered pilings hints at the bustle of shipping, logging, and commerce activity that once was Somers. A picturesque boat basin has replaced it. Many of the sailboats that now engage in racing on the lake during the year are docked here.

Finley Point, Beardance, and Woods Bay

Because the terrain along the east shore of the lake is more rugged than that along the west shore, settlement occurred more slowly. With the exception of Bigfork, located at the extreme northeast end of the lake, there are no major towns on the east shore. Settlements here include Finley Point, Woods Bay, and Beardance.

Finley Point was one of the sites chosen for the trial planting of cherry trees along the lake. In spring 1930, eight men planted several hundred Lambert cherry trees and Black Tartarian pollenizers at several sites near Polson along the south shore and around Finley Point and Skidoo Bay. These men eventually formed the Flathead Sweet Cherry Association. Today Flathead cherries are prized and abundant, with cherry stands all along Highway 35 south from Bigfork to Polson.

Henry Chapman, a displaced farmer in poor health, settled in the Beardance area in 1893, founding the Beardance Ranch. He cleared land for his cabin and an apple orchard and soon was supplying apples to markets in the East.

J. C. Woods and family became the first Woods Bay settlers in 1891. Woods planted the area's first Bing and Royal Anne cherry trees and pioneered the idea of shipping cherries to eastern markets.

Bigfork

Just north of Woods Bay is Bigfork, or Bigfork Village, as chamber of commerce personnel would like to have it called. This small, pretty town has evolved into what is essentially a seasonal resort that booms in summer and quiets down in winter. This "Village by the Bay" is considered by many to be the art center of the Flathead Valley. The Jewel Basin Hiking Area is nearby.

Located at the north end of Flathead Lake and at the mouth of the Swan River, the small town has much to offer. The main street is lined with art galleries, bars, great restaurants, unique stores, a historic hotel (offering food, not rooms), an art and cultural center, and a renowned summer playhouse. Bigfork also boasts Eagle Bend, one of the best public golf courses in the country, and a golfing-residential community. A wonderful place for families to visit is Kehoe's Agate Shop, located at 1020 Holt Drive at the north end of the Eagle Bend complex. Here you'll find a long-time family-operated shop, offering minerals, fossils, fine gems, and Montana sapphires.

For such a small place, the area can hold only a finite number of residents and still retain its charm. Some long-term residents have seen great change as "progress" and development have moved in. Some can even remember when Indians camped along the Swan River.

Bigfork's tourist season begins toward the end of May, when the Swan River begins to crest. The first event to let you know summer is coming is the Northern Rockies Paddlefest, usually held the weekend before Memorial Day at Wayfarers State Park, just south of Bigfork on Highway 35. Here you'll be able to paddle and look over all sorts of kayaks and canoes, provided by local stores and boat companies. At this event you'll get help for the beginner and advice for the more advanced (as well as the chance to purchase boats and equipment).

Then, usually on Memorial Day weekend, kayakers come from all over, eager to run what is reverentially referred to as the "Mad Mile." The celebration lasts for three days, with kayakers running different events down the raging river. As summer descends, evenings see costumed performers strolling the

Village of Bigfork—The Mad Mile

Boulders line the Swan River by Bigfork—prominent ones as well as hidden ones. About the only favorable thing that can be said about their presence is that they are generally smooth and rounded from years of rushing water.

There is a way to venture through this area between the dam on the Swan and Bigfork Bay—the area popularly referred to as the "Mad Mile" by those who have learned to negotiate it. This trip is not for everyone. Successful negotiation requires skills honed to such a fine edge that all actions come automatically, for there are many stretches that test the skills of even the most experienced white-water buffs. Waters here run from Class I through Class IV or V, depending on the heaviness of spring runoff. Running this course requires advanced to expert skill levels.

Some specific areas have received honorary designations. Consider, for example, the "Moe Hole," where Tom Moe got caught back in the 70s, lost his paddle, and had his boat broken into a dozen or more pieces. Cliff Person said it best: "The Moe Hole is treacherous. You're on the crest of a wave with the sun shining in your face and then, suddenly, you're dropped into a hole and thrashed about."

Cliff Person of Whitefish organized the first white-water Mad Mile kayak gathering in 1974. The race has come a long way since then. In 1980 the Bigfork Chamber of Commerce began a May Whitewater Festival. The annual event has proved so successful that a former Montana governor declared Bigfork "The White Water Capital of Montana."

To add spice to the event, two types of racing are included. In one, racers are timed over the entire course; the other is a slalom event, where racers must perform a number of maneuvers.

This multiday event is fun for the entire family. Contact the Bigfork Chamber of Commerce for information regarding dates and how to participate if you have the requisite skills.

Bigfork's Mad Mile is a hell-a-ceous 1-mile run during the spring runoff.

streets before they gather to perform at the Bigfork Summer Playhouse. Fall brings folks still wanting to hike or be on the lake to view the autumn colors. Winter doesn't bring in a huge influx of tourists, but they still come to Bigfork to dine and relax after a day of skiing or other winter sports. At Christmastime the Bigfork Elves decorate the streets and buildings, and the lights reflect the beauty of the season off the waters of Bigfork Harbor.

More Flathead Communities

Coram, Hungry Horse, and Martin City

Three small communities make up what is known as The Canyon. Bustling in the tourist season, they offer quiet in winter. The Canyon is full of shops, fruit (yes, huckleberry!) stands, infamous saloons, restaurants, and tourist attractions. All three towns lie along U.S. Highway 2 just south of Glacier National Park.

Established in 1914, Coram is the oldest of the three towns. Just past Coram is Hungry Horse ("Dam Town"), in existence since the 1940s. Hungry Horse Dam and Reservoir are well worth visiting. Martin City, located on the road on the east side of the dam, was also established in the late 1940s. Thousands come each year to fish and white-water raft along the Middle Fork of the Flathead River, where the corridor runs the Bad Rock Canyon

The Dams

Hungry Horse Dam

According to an often-told local story, the name Hungry Horse tells of the ordeal of two draft horses in the rugged Montana wilderness. Tex and Jerry pulled logging sleighs in the Flathead River's South Fork area. During the severe winter of 1900–1901, they wandered away from their sleigh and struggled for a month in belly-deep snow, unable to find food. They were gaunt and weak when found, prompting the observation that this was "mighty hungry horse country." Tex and Jerry were revived and the name stuck, eventually to be given to a mountain, a lake, and a creek in northern Flathead country and later to the town and dam located a short distance downstream.

The dam produces enough electricity to meet the needs of five cities the size of Missoula, Montana (population about 62,000). It also serves as an upstream storage area. Water stored upstream can be controlled to help downstream dams generate sufficient electricity to supply twenty-five cities the size of Missoula. Hungry Horse Dam has its power source in the middle of designated wilderness areas. On the west side is Jewel Basin; from the other points of the compass sprawl the Great Bear and Bob Marshall Wilderness areas. Waters from these areas are stored behind a dam that at the time of its construction was the fourth largest in the world. Today the reservoir has become a favorite for campers. A 100-mile-long paved and gravel road surrounds the reservoir and takes recreationalists to areas offering fishing, camping, and boating.

The reservoir stretches more than 35 miles through beautiful and remote country and is popular among pleasure boaters. For fishing, however, Hungry Horse Reservoir comes up lacking. The reservoir is managed for power-production purposes, and during low water, simply reaching the lake can be a challenge. Unlike most other reservoirs in Montana, the 34-mile-long Hungry Horse is not stocked. For those who want to attempt to fish the Hungry Horse Reservoir, the best place is around some of the inlets and bays all along the reservoir's shoreline. Over the years we've had luck near the Lost Johnny Campground.

At a height of 564 feet, the dam is an imposing sight. It contains 3,086,200 cubic yards of concrete and backs up water 30 miles. The dam was completed in 1951 and ready to be filled except for one last task. When the diversion tunnel was closed during construction, it trapped hundreds of fish in its 378-foot-long passage. Some of these fish were caught and released in the main river, and some were taken to the fish hatchery in Creston. Hungry Horse Dam is one of the twenty-plus dams in the Columbia River system. Call (406) 387–5241 for a tour schedule of the dam.

Hungry Horse, the Dam Town

Sixty years or so ago, this dam town was as wild and woolly as any cow town might have been at the turn of the twentieth century. Hungry Horse, to put it plainly, could be a woeful, wicked town. There were more than thirty bars, all of which reaped a good living between the late 1940s and mid-1950s, during construction of Hungry Horse Dam. Twenty thousand applicants had answered the call: "Men needed in obscure Montana setting to help build the fourth largest (at the time) dam in the world."

Kerr Dam

Few facilities or sites have drawn more attention in the Flathead and Mission Valleys than the huge concrete arch dam that blocks the Flathead River 8 miles south of Polson.

Interest in that power site dates back to prehomestead days on the Flathead Indian Reservation, home to the confederated Salish and Kootenai Tribes. The site sat untouched until 1920, when the Federal Water Power Act was enacted. For ten more years, delays and political bickering kept anything from happening until Montana Power Company was granted a permit to proceed with construction in May 1930. The dam would be named for MPC President, Frank Kerr.

Today Kerr is considered a dam of distinction. The project was the biggest private construction activity in Montana during the Great Depression of the 1930s. The canyon wall overlooking the dam provides visitors with a pleasant place to hike, an easy descent down a well-maintained step pathway with resting spots, and a challenging climb back up to the top. The area is also a jumping-off place for river rafters who wish to float the wild section known as Buffalo Rapids.

Sheep, deer—and just a few horses—still roam on Wild Horse Island.

Chapter 9
Flathead Valley Attractions

There is always something to do here and someplace to go. Even folks who are native to the valley constantly find something new and different. Here we offer a few of the major attractions, knowing that time may be a constraint. Hopefully you'll get the flavor of the valley area and come back for more—again and again.

Places to Stay and See

Izaak Walton Inn

Located in Essex on U.S. Highway 2, about 30 miles east of West Glacier, the inn is a famous landmark as well as a popular year-round inn. Once you've visited or stayed at the inn, you'll consider it a special place and will want to return often.

The inn is an old railroad hotel and still serves the railroad (Amtrak) as well as the public. Through the years, two hotels on the site have burned down. The present-day inn has twenty-two rooms and averages more than a thousand guests in the January-to-April ski season alone. Summer provides delightful hiking and good fishing. Guides for all sports are available through the inn.

The food here is truly delicious; many locals from the valley drive up here just for the experience (and the total peace and quiet). The inn hosts many events year-round and is a popular place for business meetings. For information call (406) 888–5700. The Amtrak train runs through here, picking up and dropping off passengers. On the night run everyone at the inn goes out the front door to wave the train good-bye.

Conrad Mansion

On the National Register of Historic Places and once the home of Charles Conrad, the mansion has been lovingly restored and is filled with elegant antiques. Tours are offered daily from May through October. During the Christmas season the mansion is splendidly decorated and tours are available. An interesting stone wall encircles the mansion, located on Woodland Avenue in Kalispell. Call (406) 755–2166 for information.

Hockaday Museum of Art

Located at 302 Second Avenue East in Kalispell, the museum is well worth a visit. It is open Tuesday through Saturday, with free admission on Wednesday.

The museum features changing art exhibitions and interesting programs for both adults and children. Call (406) 755–5268.

Museum at Central School

Located at 124 Second Avenue East in Kalispell, the museum is also on the National Register of Historic Places. Originally this was Kalispell's first school before becoming Flathead Valley Community College (which is now located on U.S. Highway 93, just north of town). Completely renovated in the 1990s, the building is now home to the museum and the Northwest Montana Historical Society. You'll also find meeting rooms, a cafe, and a gift shop. The museum is open Tuesday through Saturday, with a $5.00 admission fee. Call (406) 756–8381 for more information.

Bigfork Art and Cultural Center

This nonprofit community organization is located on Electric Avenue in Bigfork. Local artists have their artwork and crafts on display, and special showings are held throughout the year. Call (406) 837–6927.

While in Bigfork, as you wander Electric Avenue, stop in at the many galleries and shops offering wonderful paintings, bronze work, and crafts. In 2002 Bigfork received the Montana Tourism Community of the Year award, particularly for the "Christmas in Bigfork" celebration.

Stumptown Historical Society

Located at 500 Depot Street in Whitefish, this museum is open year-round. With free admission, it holds a wonderful history of Whitefish. Call (406) 862–0067.

Big Mountain Resort

Besides skiing in the winter months, this resort offers a warm-weather adventure called "Walk in the Tree Tops," a three-hour excursion along a canopy boardwalk 30 to 60 feet above the forest. First you ride a bike (provided) or take a shuttle 1 mile to the start of the walk. You are given a safety orientation and then don climbing harnesses and hard hats; you will be connected with lines to safety cables above the boardwalk. Views of the Flathead Valley are spectacular, and the trees below are up to 200 years old. You also may encounter wildlife below. This activity is for those over the age of ten and 54 inches or taller. The cost is about $48 per person. Take US 93 to Whitefish, then follow the signs for Big Mountain, 8 miles north of town. For reservations (recommended) call (406) 862–2900.

Miracle of America Museum and Pioneer Village

The museum is located in Polson, at the south end of Flathead Lake on US 93. It houses more than 100,000 Americana artifacts and is the largest in northwest

Janie Gildart attaches her safety hook to the line before venturing onto the "Walk in the Tree Tops."

Montana. The village has an 1890s sod-roofed log cabin and a 1912 schoolhouse. Open every day year-round. Call (406) 883–6804 for more information.

Polson Flathead Historical Museum

Located at 708 Main Street in Polson, the museum contains historical artifacts of pioneers and Indians as well as other good stuff from the Flathead Valley. The museum is open from May through September. Call (406) 883–3049.

People's Center

Located at 53253 US 93 West in Pablo (a few miles south of Polson), the center is a wonderful educational center detailing the cultures of the Salish, Kootenai, and Pend d'Oreille peoples. The center holds a gallery and a gift shop with local Indian arts and crafts and offers tours. A small admission fee is charged. Call (800) 883–5344 for more information.

Laurel Cheff preserves Indian artifacts and history at the Ninepipes Museum.

Ninepipes Museum of Early Montana

Located on US 93 just south of Pablo, this is a "must-see" museum owned by Bud and Laurel Cheff. Their incredible collection of Native American art and artifacts is hard to beat. One of their most interesting pieces is a brain-tanned deer hide with a "Winter Count" drawn on it. Long ago the Indians would gather, recount what had occurred in their lives during the preceding year, and record it on a hide. The museum store offers high-quality gifts and artifacts. A small admission fee is charged. For more information call (406) 644–3435.

St. Ignatius Mission

The mission is in the town of St. Ignatius, 70 miles south of Kalispell on US 93. A visit to the 1891 Jesuit Church is a must. The local Indians helped build this beautiful mission, and inside you'll be treated to gorgeous murals and frescoes depicting the Old and New Testaments, which were painted by a Jesuit brother. Services are still held in the mission. No admission is charged. Call (406) 745–2768.

North American Wildlife Museum

The museum is located in Coram, on US 2 West, on the way to West Glacier. Everything is right here: an RV park and campground, a gift store, and a big exhibit—life-size reproductions of animals in a natural setting. A small admission fee is charged. Call (406) 387–4018 for more information.

Native American Powwows

In summer the Flathead and the Blackfeet hold separate powwows on their respective reservations. For information on the Kootenai powwow at Elmo in July, call (406) 675–2700. The annual Blackfeet North American Indian Days celebration is held in July at Browning, which is about 10 miles south of East Glacier on US 2 East. If you get to Browning, stop in at the Museum of the Plains Indians at the junction of U.S. Highway 89 and US 2 West. Call (406) 338-2230 for additional information.

Lake Mary Ronan

Nestled in Douglas fir and western larch and surrounded by the Salish Mountains lies 1,513-acre Lake Mary Ronan, a favorite spot for locals. The fishing here is often superb, including yellow perch, largemouth bass, kokanee salmon, and rainbow trout. You can fish the lake all year (some love the ice fishing), but

The Airstream and a wall tent surround the fire, the focal point of a family gathering at Lake Mary Ronan, where Will Friedner adds a chunk of wood.

there are closure restrictions at certain times. Contact Montana Fish, Wildlife and Parks on Meridian Road in Kalispell for Montana fishing regulations and the exceptions for Lake Mary Ronan. Remember to pick up a Montana fishing license as well.

Not only are the fishing and boating wonderful, but trails abound where you can pick huckleberries in fall, watch for birds, and find wildflowers and other wildlife. Several campgrounds dot the road to the lake; the road ends at Lake Mary Ronan Lodge & Resort.

To reach this beautiful place, take US 93 south from Kalispell, driving on the west side of Flathead Lake. When you reach Dayton (nearly at the south end of the lake), you'll see the sign to the right for Lake Mary Ronan. Follow the road for 7 miles to the lake.

Snow ghosts form when clouds with high volumes of moisture drop to the earth, coating the trees with ice and snow.

High atop a windswept butte in western Montana, we watched a wildlife spectacle few are ever fortunate enough to see. Below us late-evening sun transformed stalks of summer-dried wheatgrass with a soft rose-colored glow. There, two giant bull bison backed ponderously away from each other until they stood 20 feet apart. The mammoth beasts pawed angrily at the parched grass, kicking dust high into the air and roaring like lions.

Muscles tensed; then the animals bore down on each other, crashing with such momentum that the sound of their impact carried far above the gusting wind of the sprawling plains. Again and again they repeated the ritual, colliding like locomotives until it appeared their skulls would shatter.

The brutal punishment continued for fifteen to twenty minutes. Finally, just as the sun dipped toward a distant range of peaks, one combatant turned groggily and staggered off. With eyes aglare, the other turned—defiant, angry—searching for yet another challenger. Clearly, this huge bull was king of the pasture.

We were on Montana's National Bison Range, fascinated by the power of these beasts—and appreciating the fact that this energy was now being unleashed just a few miles from the campground we always use as a base during our frequent trips to the refuge. The 8-mile drive from Willow Creek Campground to the bison range makes it ideally located, but we also like the campground because of owners Skip and Sue Palmer. Skip is a well-seasoned employee at the bison range, and with his walrus mustache and a tall Stetson hat to complement his lean appearance, obviously this man is not a paper pusher. In fact, one of Skip's roles is riding horses to drive bison during the annual fall roundup, an event we always attend. For us the roundup provides another chapter in the exciting story of bison on one of our nation's premier wildlife refuges; it is every bit as exciting as watching angry bulls engage in ritualistic contests.

Bison that inhabit today's refuge have a unique origin, dating back to spring 1873 when Walking Coyote, a Pend d'Oreille Indian, captured five bison calves. Coyote had been wintering in what is now eastern Montana, and during a hunting expedition the man separated out five calves, including one bull calf, from one of the last great herds.

Next spring Walking Coyote took the young bison to St. Ignatius Mission, located on the Flathead Indian Reservation adjacent to today's refuge. The calves were unusually tame and soon became favored pets. When the cows were

Skip Palmer (left) pushes bison from behind while other riders contain the flanks at the National Bison Range.

four years old, each dropped a calf. From that time on their numbers grew, and by 1884 the herd numbered thirty, which Walking Coyote then sold. Eventually the American Bison Society bought a portion of the herd, and it was used to stock the newly created bison range. On October 17, 1909, thirty-seven bison from the original Walking Coyote herd were released onto the 18,540-acre refuge. Today descendents of those animals compose one of the world's largest and best-managed herds, numbering 350 to 500 bison.

Because the bison were all acquired from Native Americans (at least indirectly), and because the land on which they roam might arguably be said to have been purchased from Indians at a time when they lacked business acumen, today, almost a hundred years later, local Native Americans have made a powerful and persuasive case to be involved in the management of the National Bison Range. They are involved in much of the refuge's maintenance and some interpretation.

When we visit the refuge, our first stop is always the visitor center. We never tire of viewing the beautiful panels and listening to the audio headphone interpretations, which reinforce our understanding of the role bison played in the lives of the once formidable Plains Indians. We also enjoy relearning the story of Big Medicine, an albino bison born on the range in 1933.

According to old Indians, such an event is so rare, "Even the Great Spirit is surprised to see one." Certainly that observation has held here, for although the albino bull passed his genes on to many offspring, the bison range has not seen another all-white buffalo since the passing of Big Medicine on August 25, 1959. By then, however, his presence ensured that visitation would always be substantial.

Today the number of annual visitors to the refuge approaches 200,000. Though many come for the roundup, others are more like Janie and me—coming simply to learn about bison in general and to see an intact prairie and mountain ecosystem, for bison at the refuge share their domain with a full complement of other species.

To facilitate your tour, a 19-mile-long loop road takes you through several habitat types. You can make the drive from mid-May to about the second weekend in November, depending on weather. The road is graveled, and because it contains many switchbacks, RVs over 30 feet are discouraged. Trailers and other towed units (such as boats) are not allowed, but there is a large parking lot for drop-offs. Those with tow vehicles should leave their RVs behind.

Those making the drive on this one-way road usually see wildlife within the first few miles. In spring I've photographed young antelope along an area known as Pauline Springs. About 8 miles later, the road peaks at an elevation of 4,700 feet. Here the Bitterroot Trail links with the road and proceeds for several hundred yards to the highest point in the refuge (4,800 feet). The trail is appropriately named—in late spring the hills are aglow with the soft pink petals of the bitterroot, Montana's state flower. The area is also a hangout for sheep, deer, elk, and an occasional blue grouse. Sightings of animals and flowers are all backdropped by glacier-clad McDonald Peak. At such times it's easy to see why radio commentator Paul Harvey proclaimed that one of his favorite Montana drives took him through the Mission Valley.

You'll always see bison, as you travel in the refuge, but in late July, out on the flats near the end of the drive is where you're likely to see the ritualistic battles. Once, as two of these mighty gladiators fought, we watched with astonishment as a visitor armed with his video camera, leaped from his car and ran closer for a better look—ignoring the posted signs. Although large bull bison may weigh 2,000 pounds, they can spin on a dime and can charge at speeds up to 30 miles per hour. They are temperamental beasts that insist on their space. Fortuantely nothing happened to the ignorant and inconsiderate visitor, who endangered not only himself but us as well.

Fights establish a hierarchy among the bulls, the strongest of which then breed with the cows. Young are born in spring, and by season's end the herd of about 350 to 400 has multiplied to about 700 animals. If allowed to increase unchecked, before long the herd would number in the thousands. To ensure that the limited range is not overgrazed, each fall managers conduct the roundup, essentially intended to control herd size.

Prior to the roundup, Skip Palmer and other riders have been working behind the scenes, pushing the bison to a central corral located high on a hill overlooking the processing corrals. That takes several weeks, but the riders are professionals, and the roundup almost always begins on schedule.

Typically, processing begins when a group of four to five ranch hands rides slowly toward the herd and cuts out about twenty bison—about all they can comfortably handle. They ease behind the group they've just created and quickly flank the animals. Then they spur their horses and begin directing the bison, slowly at first but then quickly, into an all-out run down to the holding pens.

Palmer says that it is almost impossible to control a herd without pushing them into a run; walking bison are unmanageable. Those that have been separated out want to go back to the main herd. To keep them from doing that, Palmer says, "You've got to out-buffalo the buffalo." That's why they run them. "Not," he explains, "because it creates drama, but because it keeps them moving in a straight line."

Of course there are always exceptions to the rule, and once Palmer found himself literally engulfed in a swirl of grunting, snorting, angry animals. "It was tense for a while," he recalls. "About all a person could do was hold tight to the reins and pray his horse remained calm."

Once the small herd is corralled into the pens, other workers process the animals. Using tin cans mounted atop long poles, employees haze the bison, moving them from one chute to another. Bison are branded and inoculated against brucellosis. Meanwhile, Palmer and the others have returned to the larger herd and have begun the process all over again. And so it goes for the next three days.

A number of bison are also separated out and sold to the highest bidder. Some are purchased for restaurants and for grocery stores; others are purchased for private use. The bison are auctioned in a sealed bid, and sale prices range from about $400 to well over $2,000. Meat from the sale usually goes to local grocery stores; we always come back with ten to twenty pounds of low-cholesterol steaks and burgers, which we then place in our trailer's freezer.

Because the riders are so practiced, roundup proceeds smoothly. This past year about twenty-five employees worked some 500 buffalo, reducing total herd numbers to about 400—the number that, based on experience, is compatible with the land. The processing serves to make the remaining bison healthier and more vigorous.

One fall day, although it was past the breeding season, we found a huge bull that was still plowing the earth with his horns. Here was a powerful animal, one so belligerent he had eluded riders. He was still challenging, and he was still defiant. Turning, he appeared to be seeking a worthy foe; we drove on, lest he misunderstand our curious stares.

Without a doubt, this bull was king of his pasture, and he was there because of a chance relationship with Walking Coyote and an embryonic government agency. We'd see the giant again next year, and undoubtedly he'd be battling another worthy foe.

This bison was just released from the holding pen after receiving inoculations.

Flathead Lake looks so cold right after the ice breaks up in the spring.

Many moons ago, raging waters flooded the Flathead Valley, drowning nearly all but a few of the chief's tribe. As the survivors fled to higher ground, the waters followed them.

Finally, all the land was covered except for one peak where a small band of Indians huddled. The chief said, "I will try to stop the water." And he asked his guardian spirit to help him.

He then shot an arrow toward the ground at the edge of the water. It barely missed the shore and floated away, as did a second. The third arrow stayed in the ground at the very edge of the waves. The water rose to the feathers but went no higher. Gradually, much of the water receded, exposing the mountains, hills, and valleys. The water that remained formed Flathead Lake.

—Flathead Tribal Legend

According to modern geologists, the features of Flathead Valley were conceived eons before the vast Rocky Mountains appeared and streams began to flow, perhaps 600 million years ago in the Precambrian era, when vast seas covered most of what is now North America.

Tens of thousands of years ago, a vast glacier moved down the Rocky Mountain Trench through Canada. When the glacier arrived in present-day Montana, a tongue crossed over the Continental Divide in what's now Glacier National Park and moved out onto the plains. It is believed that the ice depth in what is now Kalispell reached 3,000 feet. Both the Swan and Mission Mountain ranges were partially covered.

But the most significant local influence of the glacier was its development of Flathead Lake about 12,000 years ago. To do this, the mass of ice needed to scour out a basin that would hold a large quantity of water and create a dam that would impound the water. As the mass pushed forward, it left piles of earth and rock on its sides, known as moraines.

Moraines in the Flathead Valley are of two types, lateral and terminal. One terminal moraine, called the Polson Moraine, was instrumental in the creation of the lake. Originally that moraine, a giant natural dam, impounded Flathead Lake across the southern valley. Lake water overflowed the top of the moraine and promptly began cutting downward, creating a gorge and forming the southern extension of the Flathead River. This cutting action would have emptied the lake or lowered its level had the river not encountered hard rock created 300 million years previously from the vast inland seas. This rock prevented rapid drainage of the lake.

Flathead Statistics

With a full-pool surface area of 191.5 square miles, a maximum length of 27.3 miles, and a maximum width of 15.5 miles, Flathead Lake is the largest natural freshwater lake west of the Mississippi River. The mainland shoreline is 161 miles and is dotted with residential dwellings and state parks; undeveloped shoreline sections are dominated by coniferous forests, rock outcrops, and gravel beaches. About 5.5 square miles of the lake are covered by islands, the largest being Wild Horse Island (2,100 acres). Kerr Dam, near Polson, regulates the lake's water level to the south to between 2,883 and 2,893 feet above sea level. The maximum depth of the lake is 370 feet.

Studies by the Yellow Bay Biological Station show that the lake is one of the cleanest in the world. Unfortunately, since 1977 pollution has begun to deteriorate the water quality.

Twenty-five species of fish, ten of which are native to the lake, reside here. The native species are cutthroat trout, two kinds of whitefish, bull trout, redside shiner, sculpin, large-scale and longnose suckers, and peamouth and squawfish minnows.

The lake can be divided into four distinct regions based on depth. The shallow delta is located at the mouth of the Flathead River at the extreme north end of the lake and is generally less than 20 feet deep. A relatively level shelf exists on the west half of the lake. This region, which begins just beyond the steep shoreline drop-off, ranges in depth from 80 to 150 feet. A deep trough reaching depths greater than 300 feet underlies the entire eastern half of the lake. Polson Bay, at the southern end of the lake, is isolated from the main lake body by an island-dotted strait called the Narrows. Here the water is generally less than 25 feet deep and is the most extensive shallow area of the lake.

The average January surface temperature of the lake is 36 degrees, rising to 68 degrees in mid-August. The highest temperatures occur just below Kerr Dam and may rise to more than 74 degrees.

With its tremendous inflow of 8.8 million acre-feet of water from the major river tributaries, the lake's volume is still about 2.1 times greater than the annual inflow. In other words, almost half the lake volume is replaced by river water each year.

Wild Horse—An Island of America

Flathead Lake is the largest freshwater lake in the West. Recreational opportunities include boating, fishing, sailing, and commercial cruises on large vessels. Another option is a visit to Wild Horse Island State Park. Here is a brief history of the island, some insights into how it is managed, and what you may expect to see.

In 1970 the U.S. Department of the Interior published a report entitled *Islands of America*, listing what the agency considered the most significant islands in the nation. Wild Horse Island was included in this report, and as you drive U.S. Highway 93 between Polson and Kalispell, if you linger a while near the small town of Dayton, you may understand why.

Looking to the east you see an island surrounded by some of the most magnificent country in the world. Wild Horse Island is bordered to the east and north by the Swan and Mission Mountain ranges. But if there is a single romantic bone in your body, your eyes will drift toward the island. It is remote and appears as though it may never have been inhabited. But that's an illusion, because the island has a history that includes Indians, homesteaders, developers, conservationists, bighorn sheep, deer, and even wild horses.

The island's history includes a brief period of homesteading, several attempts to develop the island commercially, and the establishment of a dude ranch in 1925 that survived into the mid-1930s. Since that time the island has passed through a succession of owners, each of whom attempted something a bit different, but none of the attempts survived.

The current owner of most of the island is the State of Montana with the rest of it held privately. Montana Fish, Wildlife and Parks is the administrator and manages the island in a manner agreeable to the greatest number of people. Fish, Wildlife and Parks also must consider the management of the island's population of bighorn sheep, which are not indigenous to the place. These critters (one male and one female) were planted on Wild Horse in 1939, and the population proliferated. When biologists concur that the population is too great for the health of the sheep, a number are transplanted. The sheep are netted, checked out, and then flown, dangling from a helicopter, to another area.

The island also has a mule deer population, and some of these are huge. With no predators to speak of, the deer, the sheep, and the remaining horses enjoy the island with no fear. Today sheep number about seventy-five, deer about twenty-five, and horses, three. These animals are on the island for the enjoyment of hikers, photographers, and curiosity seekers.

For those interested in visiting this "Island of America," you may take your own personal watercraft or hook up with one of the guide services on the west shore of the lake. These include kayak companies that will provide lessons and

Periodically the sheep population mushrooms on Wild Horse Island, and some must be moved to a new location.

offer trips, as well as outfits that provide motorized access. Wild Horse Island State Park is managed for day-use only, and open fires are not permitted.

Flathead Lake Marine Trail

According to Montana Fish, Wildlife and Parks, a marine trail is a "network of access points and stopover areas for users of human- and wind-powered beachable watercraft. The sites are of sufficient number to allow the small boater to travel from one site to another in a single day."

If you are the owner of, or have access to, a canoe, sailboat, kayak, or similar craft, get on Flathead Lake and follow the Marine Trail. Remember, this lake is 30 miles long and 15 miles across at its widest point. Always check the weather forecast, and be prepared for the winds that sometimes gust, particularly later in the afternoon. Only you know the extent of your skills, and you should be mentally and physically able to meet unexpected challenges.

It's best to start out early and plan your destination carefully. Carry plenty of drinking water or a purifier. Wear a wet or dry suit, and don't travel alone. A map and compass are vital—fog sometimes rolls in, restricting vision. Carry the proper safety gear, and always wear your PFD (life jacket)!

Now that you have all the warnings (which really will make your trip safer and more enjoyable), the following should help you plan a wonderful trip. Using the foldout map at the back, you'll see that you can travel from one end of the lake to the other on the Marine Trail. There are motels, private campgrounds, and B&Bs along the shore, and the chambers of commerce in Bigfork, Lakeside, and Polson can guide you when choosing accommodations.

Big Arm, Finley Point, and Wayfarers Parks each have two marine campsites for those in beachable crafts (those that can be pulled completely out of the water). Yellow Bay Park has one marine campsite, and West Shore Park has three. Landing areas are marked by diamond-shaped signs. Open fires are not allowed at Yellow Bay. Bird Island and Cedar Island are open to the public at no charge, but they have no water or facilities. Open fires are prohibited on the islands. Cedar and Bird Islands are closed from March 1 to Memorial Day due to wildfowl nesting. Wild Horse Island is open year-round, but camping, fires, and pets are prohibited. If you're launching from the town of Rollins (on the west shore) to access Cedar Island, be sure to stop at the Painted Rocks. Here you'll find ancient pictographs, seen only from the water.

You may reserve (up to ten days in advance) one site from each park for multiday trips or as a departure point, and the sites must be in use by 6:00 P.M. Offwater folks have priority for any sites not taken, but walk-in campers can use a vacant one after 6:00 P.M. If you're from out of state, you'll need to park in dayuse areas and pay a daily vehicle fee or purchase an annual State Park Pass.

Janie Gildart kayaks in early morning light on Flathead Lake.

Montana residents pay indirectly—we pay for state-park access when we purchase a new vehicle registration.

Everyone, however, pays camping fees May through September of $15.00 per night. Montana seniors and the disabled pay $7.50 per night. From October through April fees are $2.00 less (no water or host); during this period there is a maximum of eight people and two tents per site.

For group camping permits, call (406) 751–4577 Monday through Friday from 9:00 A.M. to 4:00 P.M. For all other information contact Montana Fish, Wildlife and Parks at 490 North Meridian Road in Kalispell to obtain a map and brochure on the Marine Trail; or call (406) 752–5501.

Tributaries of the Flathead

Nature has graciously provided a method for replenishing the sparkling—and sometimes muddy—waters that flow through Flathead country. The sun transforms the Pacific Ocean's frothy surfaces into water vapor. Each energized particle rises and soon begins to coalesce with others, forming massive cloud formations that move inland. Sometimes these clouds move quickly and violently; at other times they sail quite casually over long, lazy days.

As they approach the mighty Rockies, these water-bearing clouds are compressed, ascending mountain masses along the backbone of the Rockies that rise to heights of more than 10,000 feet.

As the clouds rise, they cool and their precipitation falls on the upper reaches of Flathead country—on Glacier National Park, the Bob Marshall Wilderness, and the Great Bear Wilderness. In some locales, rain and snow provide 80 to 100 inches of water annually.

Much of the rainwater and snowmelt percolates into the soil, forming springs. At other sites, water from rain and melting snowbanks flows overland, forming tiny creeks that meander through alpine meadows. Some of these streams that follow the same path year after year have been given names. Stretching across the upper reaches of Flathead country are creeks with names like Little Salmon, Kintla, and Scalp. Soon these watercourses gather with others—growing, merging, intertwining, and intermingling as gravity draws them downward. Eventually they become the North, South, and Middle Forks of the Flathead River.

The three forks of the Flathead River receive most of their water between April and June. Warm weather, often coupled with periods of rain, initiates the surge of spring runoff. Stream levels can rise very rapidly from April through mid-May, and peak flows often exceed ten times the average flow. During 1964 heavy rains on top of an above-normal snowpack brought record flows to the North and Middle Forks and the larger Flathead River, causing extensive flooding in the upper Flathead River Valley. Flows on the Middle Fork rose to nearly fifty times their annual average. In Glacier National Park, McDonald Creek ran upstream. U.S. Highway 2 across from the airport was underwater, and the flood kept going into the small area of Evergreen.

But that was an unusual year. Normal high flows generally provide excellent white-water rafting for four to six weeks, with the runoff beginning to taper by mid-June. Stream flows drop steadily throughout the summer.

The three forks of the Flathead are widespread and drain vast areas. They contribute more than 90 percent of the upper Flathead River's flow. The Stillwater and Whitefish Rivers are the most important tributaries downstream from the point where the three northern forks merge. The annual flow into the upper Flathead River—before it enters Flathead Lake—averages 7.6 million acre-feet. The Swan River contributes another 880,000 acre-feet of water directly to Flathead Lake at Bigfork.

North Fork Access

The North Fork arises in southeastern British Columbia, where it is called the Flathead River. At the border its name changes to the North Fork of the Flathead. The river can be easily accessed in the following places: from the Canadian

The North Fork of the Flathead River, about to be engulfed in winter, forms a boundary between Glacier National Park and the Flathead National Forest.

border, from the bridge over the North Fork between the Polebridge Mercantile and the Polebridge Ranger Station, from the bridge providing access to Glacier National Park at the Camas entrance, from the campground at Big Creek, and and from Blankenship Bridge.

Middle Fork Access

The Middle Fork originates at the northern end of the Bob Marshall Wilderness and flows in a general northwesterly pattern through the Great Bear Wilderness. Below its junction with Bear Creek, the river follows most of the southern boundary of Glacier National Park. Numerous tributaries feed the river from both sides. One of these, McDonald Creek, drains the 6,800-acre Lake McDonald in Glacier National Park.

The Middle Fork can be accessed from where Bear Creek converges with the Middle Fork, from the Paola Creek campground, from Moccasin Creek, and from the West Glacier Bridge.

South Fork Access

The South Fork originates at the southeast end of the Bob Marshall Wilderness and runs through the heart of it before entering 39-mile-long Hungry Horse Reservoir, formed by 564-foot-high Hungry Horse Dam. There are two accesses. This first one is quite difficult, but folks do it! Leave the Swan Valley by foot or horseback from Gordon Pass, which is at Holland Lake, about 10 miles south of Condon, Montana, on Highway 83, accessed just north of Bigfork. It is 35 miles to the source of the South Fork River in the Bob Marshall Wilderness, a two-day horse trip or a two- to three-day hike. For the second, easier option: Drive around Hungry Horse Dam (just north of the town of Hungry Horse, east of Columbia Falls on Highway 2) from either the west or east side entrance. Follow a dirt road about 50 miles until you reach the bridge over Meadow Creek Gorge, your access point. This is where the South Fork is released by Hungry Horse Reservoir.

Flathead River Access

Access points for the Flathead River (from confluence of the river's three forks near Hungry Horse to head of Flathead Lake) include:

Teakettle: Access in Columbia Falls on US 2.

Kokanee Bend: Access is 3 miles south of Columbia Falls on the east side of the river; can be accessed from the Columbia Falls Stage Road.

Presentine Bar: Access is midway between Columbia Falls and Kalispell on US 2. Look for the Birch Grove Road and turn east.

Old Steel Bridge: Access by taking Conrad Drive east from Kalispell.

Leisure Island: Access from Leisure Drive by taking Conrad Drive east, then Willow Glen Drive south from Kalispell.

County Launch: From the Creston Firehall, drive 4 miles south on River-side Road to Ranchettes Road. Turn right and go 0.25 mile to T intersection. Turn right and follow the road to the river.

Therriault Road: From the Creston Firehall, drive 4.5 miles south on Riverside Road past Ranchettes to Therriault Road, a dirt road. Turn right. This access is not for large boats; turnaround is restricted. We can just manage with our 20-foot johnboat.

The Lower River (the "Forgotten Flathead")

After circulating through the lake, the waters from the high ground of Flathead country exit the lake from the southwest side of Polson Bay, then pass through the old river channel and Kerr Dam. After passing through the dam, the waters once again resume their southward course as a river.

Called by some the "Forgotten Flathead," the lower Flathead River stretches almost 70 miles between the dam and the river's confluence with the Clark Fork River near Paradise, Montana. Relatively inaccessible to the public, these 70 miles have only four access points: at Buffalo, Sloan's Bridge, Dixon, and Perma. This portion of the river drains 156,358 acres and is a low-gradient river. As it meanders south and west, it picks up water from four tributaries and at its mouth annually discharges 259.5 cubic yards per second. This is one of the largest rivers in Montana.

Because this section of the river runs through the Flathead Indian Reservation, you must purchase a special-use tribal permit. To float this section you will want to put in at Sloan Bridge and then take out near Dixon. If you plan to fish, you will need a tribal permit and a Montana fishing license to do so.

Chapter 12
Floating the Rivers

Middle Fork

Spruce Park, a section of Montana's 60-mile-long Middle Fork of the Flathead River, is a river rat's delight. This several-mile-long stretch of water is laced with sinkholes, standing waves, whirlpools, and hundreds of boulders that challenge equipment and a rafter's skills. There's no gradual easing into the frothing waters here. Suddenly the river grips oarsmen in its brawny hold. Water punches over bows, whirling crafts in eddies and then thrusting them back into the major force of the current.

Typically those who float the Middle Fork are drawn to it because of its wilderness characteristics, as seen in abundance in the upper portions of this river. Here the river passes through the Great Bear Wilderness, which is nestled between Glacier National Park and the Bob Marshall Wilderness. Fishing remains superb.

Through the 1970s, the Great Bear represented an emotionally charged battleground between those for and those against endowing the area with wilderness status. The proponents won, and today the Great Bear remains pristine, protecting a river whose headwaters are as interesting to reach as the river is exciting to navigate. In fact, some say the Middle Fork is one of the most exhilarating rivers in the Northwest.

If you're toting a hundred-pound raft and assorted gear, the headwaters of the Middle Fork can be reached only by pack animal or light plane. If time is of the essence, check out one of the local aviation companies in Kalispell for a flight to Schafer Meadow—a small grass-covered airstrip that was grandfathered into the wilderness. Before descending between snow-covered mountains, your pilot will circle the strip to be sure it is clear of moose. After landing you'll load your gear into USDA Forest Service wheelbarrows, available from nearby Schafer Ranger Station.

Because you are approaching the headwaters of the Middle Fork, water generally will be low even in June, the best time to go. But as the day progresses, the Middle Fork picks up volume from Schafer, Morrison, and Granite Creeks, then from Castle, Lunch, and Long Creeks too. Still, the Middle Fork remains relatively calm; other than the kaleidoscope of landscape, the only significant change is the boulders' sizes. They are huge, and if you're making the trip in late June or early July, you'll be doing lots of pushing and pulling over boulders and sandbars. Nevertheless, if you are a fisherman, you won't be disappointed on any account.

One attraction of floating the upper section of the Middle Fork is that your trip could be a leisurely one. From Schafer Meadow to the take-out point at Bear Creek is a distance of only about 30 miles. On a five-day jaunt, that leaves time for hiking a few of the many trails that weave throughout the Great Bear. Keep your eyes open for bears—both black and grizzly—quenching their thirst, stalking the river's shores, or angling for fish in their own particularly direct and efficient manner.

The Great Bear also preserves a variety of other species; more than likely, you'll see elk and a variety of birds associated with pristine waters. One intriguing bird is the water ouzel, or dipper. This species protects its young by constructing nests in only the wildest of areas—behind waterfalls or along the banks of raging rivers.

Although water flows are relatively smooth (except for the Three Fork Series), pay close attention to your map for Morrison Creek. Here's where the waters really begin to change. Look near Morrison Creek for a log cabin perched on a platform of rocks. In the historic 1964 flood, waters uprooted the cabin and sent it careening downstream, where it lodged 20 feet higher than the area through which you'll float. The cabin is a visual reminder of the power of water, and the spot provides an audio reminder of what lies ahead. Listen and you'll hear the roar of water emanating from the canyon just below. Prepare for the rapids through the area known as Spruce Park, which under the right circumstances contain Class V waters, all depending on runoff.

Much of the river's wildness here is the result of its steep gradient. The river drops an average of 34 feet per mile from its headwaters to Bear Creek. Through the Spruce Park area, a 4-mile section of the stream drops an average 41 feet per mile. This section is the one so anticipated by white-water enthusiasts.

As you approach the area, look for a tortuous bend in a narrow canyon where water gushed into the side of a wall and then folded back on itself. A relatively short stretch downstream, you'll get relief from the turbulence in the form of a sandy beach. Paddle vigorously for that opening, and plan on pulling over. Use this area to evaluate the waters below you; if you don't feel comfortable, then line your raft through this area.

When we paddled the area, the waters, although rough, were not violent and we decided to plunge on. Orienting our raft so that the bow pointed upstream, we paddled against the current, pulling with all our strength, trying to counter the surging water and avoid having it slam us into the cliff's face. Although our passage was successful, it was not particularly artful—we grazed the side, shipping a bit of water.

The distance from Spruce Park to the take-out point at Bear Creek near U.S. Highway 2 is about 8 miles. The river continues at this confluence, forming the southwestern boundary for Glacier National Park. For 40 more miles, the Middle Fork flows freely, passing incredibly spectacular country. Still, this section is not a wilderness river. That designation is appropriate only for the upper portion, where two sections combine to form a great unified corridor—that portion where humans must revolve their thinking around fish, bears, and unpredictable waters.

When You Go

You don't need to own sophisticated rafting equipment to enjoy any segment of the Middle Fork. If you don't own such equipment, we strongly recommend that you take a trip with one of the local commercial raft companies (see appendix A). In this manner you can determine if rafting is a sport in which you'd like to invest several thousand dollars. We joined Onno Wieringa, one of the owners of the Glacier Raft Company, and then picked his brain for information. He invites others to do the same—to learn techniques based on his thirty-five years of rafting in many parts of the Northwest.

Wieringa believes that a good-quality raft about 14 to 15 feet long is ideal for handling most waters found in the Northwest. He uses a rowing frame and can provide recommendations regarding specific features. Ours is made by Mad Dog Waterworks and is sold locally. Wieringa also uses specialized oars that break apart.

Wieringa's rafting insights can be obtained in an afternoon, but it could be much more fun to join a group for a several-night trip. Trips offered by the Glacier Raft Company range from morning and afternoon trips to a fully catered four-day trip. On such excursions, you only need to bring your personal gear, such as a sleeping bag and lots of dry clothing. For more information, call (406) 888–5541 or (800) 332–9995.

South Fork

The South Fork gathers its clear summer waters from the spring snowmelt off the lofty mountains that grace the Bob Marshall Wilderness. The fork officially begins where the Danaher River joins Gordon Creek. The location is remote; consequently, logistics can be a problem, particularly when you wish to transport large rafts to the source. Nevertheless, there are two reasons to find ways to overcome the problems—incredible scenery and fishing that at times simply cannot be surpassed. Says biologist Bruce May, now retired from Montana Fish, Wildlife and Parks, "The area may contain the best native westslope cutthroat trout population found in the United States."

Two avenues of access are available. One leaves the Swan Valley and goes over Gordon Pass and is accessed at Holland Lake, located about 10 miles south of Condon. The other requires a long drive around Hungry Horse Dam along a rutted, dusty dirt road that stretches more than 50 miles on either the west or east side. The road twists, turns, and grinds its way around the immense reservoir behind Hungry Horse Dam. Finally you reach the bridge over Meadow Creek Gorge and your access point. If you're packing a raft, you'll need help transporting it to the headwaters of the South Fork—located deep in the Bob Marshall Wilderness. Such help is available by prior arrangement at places such as the Wilderness Guest Ranch. Big Prairie Ranger Station is 35 miles away—about a two-day horse-pack trip.

As soon as you arrive, it's virtually impossible not to assemble those fly rods and begin fishing, particularly if pools are dimpled. Flies that seem to work well include the Joe Hopper and the Royal Coachman. Peak fishing season normally occurs about the middle of August, but in years of low runoff, the peak may occur two weeks earlier.

The confluence of the Danaher and Gordon provides a lovely setting; you may want to linger and make a few day hikes. Try fishing the Danaher, which can at times be exceptional. The scenery is outstanding, surrounded by the Cayune, Butcher, and Flatiron Mountains.

Eventually you'll have to push on. A leisurely float back requires about four days. While floating you will at times be amid the roar of small rapids and then beautiful pools, but nothing that will cause you to catch your breath. That comes toward your trip's end—at Meadow Creek Gorge.

Rafting Meadow Creek Gorge

About 3 miles before the parking lot, floaters encounter a sign cautioning them to take out, because of "impassable waters." In our experience, however, that's not always the case, particularly in late summer. If you have a discerning eye, you can evaluate the conditions on the way in to Big Prairie. Once we did just that and, finding the waters acceptable, decided to float the rapids. There's no law against it; you simply have to be committed to the possibility of lots of work. This is definitely one place where you should consider the passage from the Good Book that cautions: "Know thyself!"

The following relates how my fifteen-year-old son and I and two teacher friends rafted our way through Meadow Creek Gorge.

About 100 yards below the take-out sign, we encountered swift water, so we lined our way down the river. Farther along we again found more rough water and again lined down the river. But at this point our efforts proved unnecessary; we were being overly cautious.

For about half a mile we floated on—very peacefully, very placidly—until we again heard the roar of water. Climbing a rock wall, we scouted the area. No huge boulders protruded above the surface of the water, and the stretch appeared floatable. Beyond that we saw turquoise water that appeared deeper than any we'd previously encountered. Could this be the place where the canyon narrows so drastically that you can literally step across the river, the raging South Fork that elsewhere stretches almost 100 yards wide? We floated on.

Another 100 yards along, the sides of the canyon are deeply fluted, the result of the abrasive action of sand and gravel. Holes appear in the rocks where violent spring runoff has apparently swirled like a tornado, scouring out the recesses.

As we raised our eyes, the canyon walls extended above us for 300 to 400 feet. Gray-colored stone caps the higher reaches of the canyon, melding with soil and the root tendrils of majestic trees. The area is one of sublime beauty. It is unfortunate that so much discouraging literature has been published describing the river as "not navigable," for on this late-summer day that wasn't the case. Navigation does require skill, however—the ability to line a raft through fast-moving waters, a basic knowledge of rafting—and the patience to occasionally remove everything from the raft and portage it around a potential hazard.

Toward the end of the passage through the gorge, there is one place where the canyon is so narrow that you must flip your raft on its side and shove it through the rocks.

The most challenging white water is beneath the bridge that crosses the gorge, not far from the parking lot. From half a mile above, floaters can hear the roar of the waters slicing their way beneath the bridge. The high walls of the canyon create a multitude of echoes that cause the water to sound so violent, and initially the incessant roar is frightening.

At this point there are three alternatives: (1) Lash down all gear, readjust life jackets, and point the raft downstream; (2) abandon the raft and walk along the shore upstream until you find a trail; or (3) lug the raft back upstream and out of the water up a steep slope. We chose the first alternative.

Immediately downstream from the bridge, the canyon takes a nearly 90-degree turn. The water crashes against the side of the wall just below the point where the canyon turns. Rafts helplessly follow the raging current, making it impossible to avoid contact with the sheer sides of the wall. Rowing against the current to slow the velocity of the raft did not prevent us from colliding with the wall, but a few quick sweeps of the paddles pulled us away from danger. About a mile later, we reached our take-out point. My son and I concluded that, other than the work of unloading the raft to turn it on its side, the trip that year was comparable to floating through the Spruce Park area of the Middle Fork.

North Fork

Late-evening sun glistened off the gunwales of the canoe as we began our entry into the area called Fools Hen Rapids. A quick sweep with the paddle and we were around one boulder, but we had shipped a lot of water. Another sweep and more water accumulated. Soon we had to pull to the nearest bank, dump our load of water, and begin again. We explored a small portion of the river, exiting at Blankenship Bridge. Nearby was a pullout and our waiting car.

That is much the way that many people explore the North Fork of the Flathead River—in snatches. A crude logging road parallels the river, although there are some areas where you can find solitude, fishing, history, ranger stations, and a quaint country store. It all depends on the manner in which you wish to explore the area and which side of the river you choose.

The North Fork begins in Canada and enters the United States to form a boundary for Glacier National Park. Just south of the border is the old Kishinen Ranger Station—one of the earliest to be constructed in the park. To reach the station you must first locate the correct trail and then hike a short distance.

Those who find the station should attempt to imagine what life might have been like for rangers who patrolled this area in the park's early years. In those times the station was manned on a year-round basis. There was no road, and although some rangers enjoyed the isolation, others could not cope, sometimes with tragic consequence.

As the story goes, one ranger telephoned his supervisor and asked for permission to leave the area "immediately." He was despondent and emphasized that if permission were not granted "he could not be held accountable for his actions."

In response to his plea, the chief ranger told him to "get back to work," which the chief intended as constructive advice. But there was no response to the chief's suggestion—only a wintry silence ensued, shattered moments later by the sound of a gunshot over the phone.

Farther downriver—or along the road—you'll find brighter memories at the Polebridge Mercantile, which for many years hosted an annual North Fork hoedown. The store contains mounts of various animals and sells wonderful home-baked cookies as well as staples.

Downstream from the Polebridge store is the Camas Creek Bridge—a popular spot for canoeists and rafters to enter the river. To the east, Huckleberry Mountain looms. Perched atop this mountain is one of Glacier National Park's last manned lookouts, which motorists or floaters can see from several locations along the road. In 1976 this area was the site of one of the park's most massive fires. Flames leaped across Camas Creek Road and climbed the steep flanks of the mountain toward the lookout. The fireguard was evacuated and the lookout covered with protective chemicals dropped from a plane. Following the fire, vegetation came flooding back, as it often does in burned-over areas. Today the area is covered with succulent huckleberries that attract one of the densest concentrations of grizzly bears in the United States. Researchers flying over the mountains slopes frequently have reported seeing more than twenty bears during the course of a brief helicopter flight.

Farther downstream are Fools Hen Rapids. Here the stream's gradient increases and the water becomes more turbulent. Although the area is challenging and fun to float, boaters should expect a dunking. On hot summer days, this is not a major concern if boats have no cargo—they can be quickly righted.

The Lower River

To float any portion of the Flathead below Kerr Dam, called Buffalo Rapids, you'll need a tribal permit, which you can purchase from Fish, Wildlife and Parks or from sporting good stores such as Snappy's Sport Senter or the Sportsman, both in Kalispell.

Buffalo Rapids is a wild, wild section below Kerr Dam where my dad was flipped and lost his hearing aid (luckily he carried another in the onboard ammo box) and where my son David and nephew Joel named one section "the whirling pool of fear." Still, if you love white-water rafting, it's a section you've got to float, and it can be completed in an afternoon.

From U.S. Highway 93 South out of Kalispell, travel to Polson. Immediately after crossing Polson Bridge, turn right onto State Road 354. Go about 5 miles and turn right onto Dam Road; take the next right to the river, just below Kerr Dam. Float to Buffalo Bridge for about 10 miles.

If you don't want to run the rapids, you can make a three-day trip from Buffalo Bridge to Dixon. To access the Buffalo Bridge, just before the Polson Bridge on US 93, turn right onto Irvine Flats Road (a dirt road) and go about 12 miles. Turn left onto Buffalo Bridge Road and go about 5 miles to Buffalo Bridge, where you can put in below the rapids.

The Middle Fork of the Flathead River adopts an attitude as it flows through Great Bear Wilderness Area.

Where can I go now and view nature undisturbed?
—John James Audubon, 1846

Late one evening in a not-so-remote area of the Bob Marshall Wilderness, I stood with a group of young men from a local Boy Scout troop and watched as a herd of about twenty elk materialized. Then they were gone, disappearing into the rapidly descending gloom of night.

Next morning at the crack of dawn, our curiosities aroused, we ambled down to the bank were our elk had been. We found tracks made by what appeared to have been a small black bear—nothing really dramatic but nevertheless a reminder that we had seen something special, something generally seen only in the wilderness.

We've had many similar experiences in our years of wandering through Montana's wilderness areas—a cow elk swimming across a lake in the Jewel Basin Wilderness Area, a porcupine rubbing its quills along the side of our tent in the wee hours of the morning, grizzlies running free in Glacier National Park. The point is that it's still possible, even in the wake of twenty-first-century technology, to enjoy experiences that John Audubon was searching for back in 1846. We can have these opportunities primarily because Congress decreed in 1964 that a number of areas should be set aside as wilderness. Venture into them and you take home indelible memories that can be recalled when the burdens of civilization weigh heavy.

There are at least five different wilderness areas immediately adjacent to the Flathead Valley or within a few hours' drive: the Mission Mountains, Jewel Basin Hiking Area, the Bob Marshall Wilderness, the Cabinets, and the Great Bear Wilderness. All offer fair to excellent fishing, wildlife encounters, and unsurpassed opportunities to view and photograph spectacular scenery.

Perhaps the simplest way to get to these areas is by backpacking, and this is how we generally go. But there are also a number of day-hike options. The following are some of our favorites.

Northwest Montana is one of the most beautiful areas in our country. Here you'll find greatly varying terrain—from marshes and luxuriant forests filled with evergreens and ferns to sparkling clear lakes and trails that take you to the tops of mountains with truly "Big Sky" views.

Hiking is not confined to Glacier National Park. Flathead Valley is surrounded by the Swan Range of the Rockies to the east, the Columbia Range and the national park to the north, and the Salish Mountains to the west. These areas are filled with hiking trails—some difficult, some easy. Glacier National Park is often crowded in summer, especially on holidays and weekends, so here we offer some alternative suggestions for wonderful hikes, both short and long.

As noted in appendix C, take appropriate clothing, food and water, a good map, and a can of bear spray (know how to use it). Bears live in most areas of northwest Montana and sometimes want to share the hiking trails. (Bears take the easy way, too.)

Never overestimate your ability to hike a certain distance; always turn back when the trail seems too long and arduous.

Last, but never least, practice Zero Impact principles:

1. Pack it in and pack it out.
2. Properly dispose of what you cannot pack out (dig a cat hole for waste).
3. Stay on the trail.
4. Leave what you find.
5. Plan and be prepared, and let someone know of your plans.

And now, on to those promised hikes.

Whitefish Range

The Danny On Trail

Located on Big Mountain in Whitefish, this trail is named for a popular photographer and environmentalist. Danny was killed in 1979 in a ski accident on Big Mountain, but he is remembered fondly by all who knew him. The trail is an appropriate testimony to what he enjoyed.

The 7.6-mile round-trip hike is considered moderate. However, when you reach the top you can take the chairlift back down (for free) for a 3.8-mile trek. Of course you can always take the chairlift up and hike down.

Take U.S. Highway 93 into Whitefish. At the Central School, follow the signs for Big Mountain; drive to the top, and then go to the Hellroaring Saloon (near chairlift #1). The trailhead is located close to the main chairlift.

On this hike you'll travel near streams and through the woods and up a ridge, finally reaching the summit, surrounded by meadows. Here you'll have wonderful views of Glacier National Park. As always, be bear-aware in this area in late summer—the critters love the berries growing here.

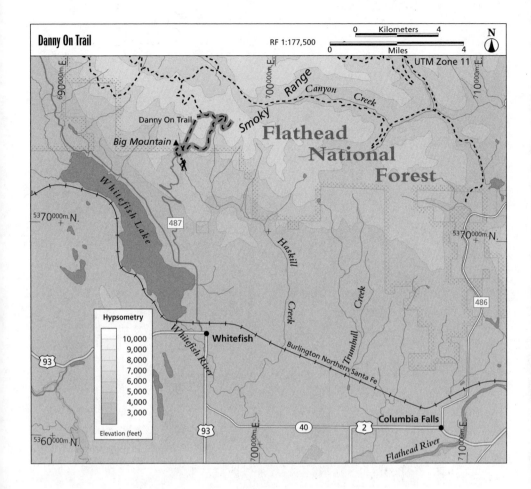

RF 1:177,500

Kilometers

Miles

N

UTM Zone 11

Smoky Range

Canyon Creek

Danny On Trail

Big Mountain

Flathead National Forest

Whitefish Lake

487

Haskill Creek

Trumbull Creek

486

Hypsometry

10,000
9,000
8,000
7,000
6,000
5,000
4,000
3,000

Elevation (feet)

Whitefish River

Whitefish

Burlington Northern Santa Fe

93

93

40

2

Columbia Falls

Flathead River

Salish Mountains

Tally Lake Trail

Tally Lake overlook is a beautiful, easy 2.5-mile round-trip option for the entire family. You'll hike through the woods, finally to emerge overlooking Tally Lake. Almost 500 feet deep, Tally is the deepest lake in Montana.

Take US 93 north from Kalispell toward Whitefish. Turn left at the light onto West Reserve Drive (just past the college), and go 4 miles to Twin Bridges Road. After about 2 miles turn right onto Farm-to-Market Road, on which you'll go about 9 miles. Turn left onto Tally Lake Road; drive through and past the campground to the parking lot and trailhead on your left.

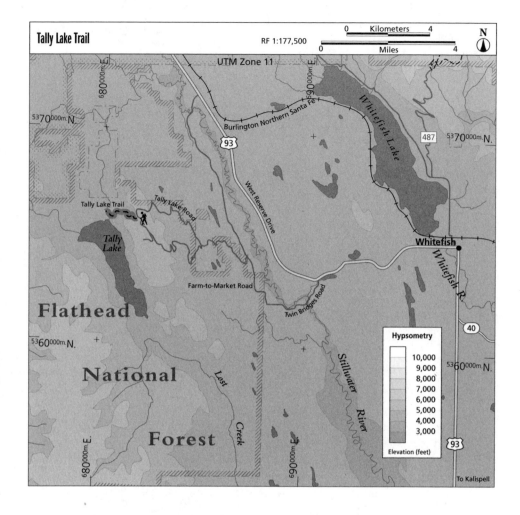

RF 1:177,500

Kilometers

Miles

N

UTM Zone 11

Burlington Northern Santa Fe

93

Whitefish Lake

487

Tally Lake Trail

Tally Lake Road

West Reserve Drive

Tally Lake

Whitefish

Flathead

Farm-to-Market Road

Twin Bridges Road

Whitefish R.

40

National

Lost Creek

Stillwater River

Hypsometry

10,000
9,000
8,000
7,000
6,000
5,000
4,000
3,000

Elevation (feet)

Forest

93

To Kalispell

The Lupine Lake Trail

The Lupine Lake Trail is about 30 miles west of Kalispell in the Salish Mountains. This easy 5-mile round-trip is fun for a family outing.

From Kalispell take U.S. Highway 2 West for 20 miles to the town of Marion; there take a right onto Little Bitterroot Lake Road. Follow this road until you come to Forest Road 538; take a right, and go 9.6 miles to the trailhead (Trail 210) on your right.

The trail drops to Griffin Creek, where there is a bridge (no need to wade) and then goes through the forest. When you reach a fork after about 1 mile, go right, up the hill; soon you're on a ridge. Then it's just a small stroll up to the lake, where you can wade, swim, or fish (with a Montana license). Retrace your steps to the trailhead.

Salish Range Parks

Two parks in the Kalispell area lie within the Salish Range. Both are delightful places to take short hikes in relative quiet.

Herron Park

Herron Park is about 5 miles west of Kalispell. Take US 2 West from Kalispell to a four-way light by Albertson's grocery. Take a left onto Meridian Road, which becomes Foys Canyon Road. Go 5 miles and take a right onto Oftedahl Lane. The parking lot will be on your left and the trails on your right. This is actually private land, owned by the Plum Creek Timber Company. There is clear evidence of logging and thinning here, but the area is still beautiful. Hike the easy trails for as long as you wish. Some folks sled and snowshoe, even cross-country ski here in winter.

Lone Pine State Park

Lone Pine State Park is in the same vicinity as Herron Park. Follow the above directions to Foys Canyon Road and go 3 miles to Foys Lake, where you'll see a sign for Lone Pine. Turn left onto Lone Pine Road and wind upward to the end of the road.

From this 229-acre park you'll have a wonderful panorama of Flathead Valley and the surrounding mountains. It is said that once a lone pine stood guard on the cliffs here and was a marker for folks going north through the valley. To reach the overlook, hike across the bridge by the visitor center and ascend to the overlook. There are four hiking-only trails here, some leading downhill for hikes of nearly 2 miles. Kids love the challenge of winning a race back up to the park. Check in at the Interpretive Center (406–755–2706) for maps, information, and activities.

Recently it has been discovered that dwarf mistletoe and a bark-beetle infestation are killing the Douglas fir and western larch trees in the park. It is hoped that ongoing restoration will halt the damage by thinning and removing some trees.

Plan to spend some time walking, relaxing, or having a picnic in this pretty park—it's a great place to relax and explore. Leashed dogs are permitted in the park.

Bigfork Area

The Swan River Nature Trail

The Swan River Nature Trail is a delightful 4-mile round-trip walk or bike ride along the Swan River in Bigfork. Take Highway 35 into the village of Bigfork and go behind Electric Avenue to access the gated trail. In spring, when the

Swan River is roaring with white water, brave kayakers run the Mad Mile down this river. Spring is also the time to see loads of wildflowers. Small paths sporadically lead down to the river. You can walk to the small dam across the river and to the bridge, where you'll reach the 2-mile mark and your turnaround point.

Sprunger-Whitney Nature Trail

Just "down the Swan" from Bigfork in an old-growth forest is a great, easy 2-mile round-trip hike called the Sprunger-Whitney Nature Trail. The area is filled with many species of birds for you bird-watchers. Elmer Sprunger is an artist; both he and Jack Whitney have been wonderful spokesmen for the environment throughout their long lives. Take Highway 35 from Kalispell south toward Bigfork. At the three-way light just before Bigfork, turn left onto Highway 83 and go to the town of Swan Lake. From there go about 7 miles to the sign on the right for the Point Pleasant Campground; turn in and follow the signs for the trailhead. Enjoy!

Swan Range

The Swan Range lies to the east of the Flathead Valley, not far off Highway 35, which runs north-south between Kalispell and Bigfork. In this range is the Jewel Basin Hiking Area, a spectacular spot to explore with 35 miles of trails. Here you'll find high alpine lakes, wildlife, and glorious scenery. Snow lingers a long while on these mountains, and sometimes the road is still snow clogged in June. Call the Flathead National Forest at (406) 758–5200 to check on road conditions.

To access the Jewel Basin, take Highway 83 east off Highway 35, about 1.5 miles north of Bigfork (this is a right turn off Highway 35 North). Go about 3 miles to Echo Lake Cafe (great breakfast and lunch year-round) on your left; turn left here onto Echo Lake Road. Go about 3 miles to a T junction and stay right, following the signs for Jewel Basin. This road becomes Jewel Basin Road (State Road 5392). The very narrow, windy (trailers not advised) dirt-gravel road climbs about 7 miles (the last 5 miles are very steep) to a parking lot and a Forest Service/ranger cabin. The lot is sometimes referred to as "Camp Misery."

As you'll see from your map, there are many trails in Jewel Basin. You can't miss on any one of them. The following are just a sample.

Camp Misery to Mount Aeneas

Camp Misery to Mount Aeneas is a 6-mile round-trip hike with an elevation gain of 1,800 feet. Although the hike is considered by some to be moderate to strenuous, take heart—there are many flat places where you can take a break and enjoy the incredible vistas.

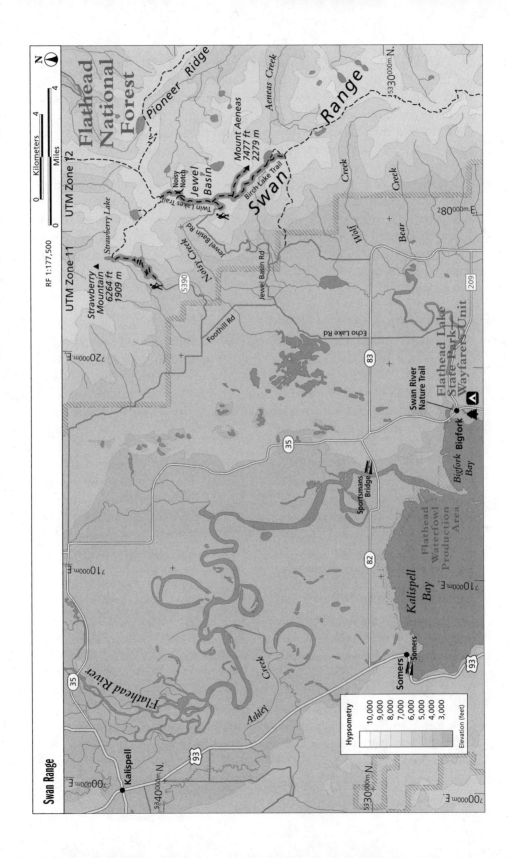

Swan Range

RF 1:177,500

Kilometers
0   4

Miles
0   4

UTM Zone 11 | UTM Zone 12

Flathead
National
Forest

Pioneer Ridge

Strawberry Mountain
6264 ft
1909 m

Strawberry Lake

Noisy Notch

Jewel Basin

Mount Aeneas
7477 ft
2279 m

Swan Range

Twin Lakes Trail

Birch Lake Trail

Aeneas Creek

5390

Noisy Creek

Jewel Basin Rd

Foothill Rd

Wolf Creek

Bear Creek

280000m.E

5330000m.N.

Echo Lake Rd

83

209

Swan River Nature Trail

Flathead Lake State Park
Wayfarers Unit

Bigfork

Bigfork Bay

720000m.E

710000m.E

270000m.E

35

Sportsmans Bridge

Flathead Waterfowl
Production Area

Kalispell Bay

82

Flathead River

Ashley Creek

Somers

Somers

93

Kalispell

35

93

700000m.E

5340000m.N.

5330000m.N.

Hypsometry

10,000
9,000
8,000
7,000
6,000
5,000
4,000
3,000

Elevation (feet)

The trailhead to Mount Aeneas is located to the left of the ranger cabin. At the first fork in the trail (about 0.5 mile), take a right, following the sign to Birch Lake. After another 0.5 mile through a spruce forest, the trail forks again. Go to the right and soon you'll be on a ridge with great views of Flathead Lake. Here the trail splits in several directions; take the left trail, which is marked TRAIL # 717. Now the path steadily climbs for about 1 mile, offering more wonderful views.

Finally you emerge from bushes onto a ridge, where you'll encounter a microwave tower. Follow the trail to the right from the tower for about 0.5 mile and there you are on top, with a 360-degree panorama. On clear days you'll see Glacier National Park, the Bob Marshall Wilderness, and the Flathead Valley and Flathead Lake. On windless days it's a great place for a picnic. Retrace your steps from here, or following the map, hike down to the Picnic Lakes to make a loop back to your vehicle. (There are no fish in the Picnic Lakes.)

Camp Misery to Twin Lakes

Camp Misery to Twin Lakes is an easy to moderate hike of 5 miles with an elevation gain of 770 feet if you follow Trail #8 up through Noisy Notch. The trailhead is to the left of the ranger cabin. When you reach the top of Noisy Notch (2.5 miles), you'll come to a T in the trail, with the Twin Lakes (no fish) right below you. Backtrack from here, or take Trail #721 (to your right) and make a loop down to the parking lot.

Camp Misery to Birch Lake

Camp Misery to Birch Lake is a 6-mile round-trip moderate hike with an elevation gain of 610 feet. Follow the hike for Mount Aeneas (above) until you reach the point where the trail branches off on Trail #717. At this point, take the far right trail, marked TRAIL #7 all the way to Birch Lake. You can hike around this beautiful alpine lake and sometimes catch cutthroat and rainbow trout. Retrace your steps from here.

Strawberry Lake

Just northwest of the Jewel Basin area is a wonderful little lake, Strawberry, sitting at the base of Strawberry Mountain. It's not part of Jewel Basin, but it's just as pretty, and the moderate 6-mile out-and-back hike is great for the whole family.

To access this area, take Highway 83 toward Swan Lake from Highway 35, just north of Bigfork. Go 3 miles and turn left at the Echo Park Cafe onto Echo Park Road. You'll come to a T junction in about 2 miles; make a left onto Foothills Road and travel until you reach Forest Road 5390 on your right. Follow this road until its end, where you can park and access the trailhead.

The trail begins by climbing (about 1,500 feet total elevation gain) through a spruce-fir forest. Toward the end you'll break out of the woods and go through a pretty notch to the lake. We've seen folks pull small fish from here. We've also seen some not-too-tired people climb Strawberry Mountain, directly to the east.

Columbia Mountain

This is a difficult 6.5-mile one-way hike to the top of Columbia Mountain (elevation 7,208 feet). If you go on a clear day, the views are well worth the effort. The trek begins at the valley bottom and switches back and forth across the west face of the mountain on Forest Service lands in the Hungry Horse Ranger District (406–387–3800).

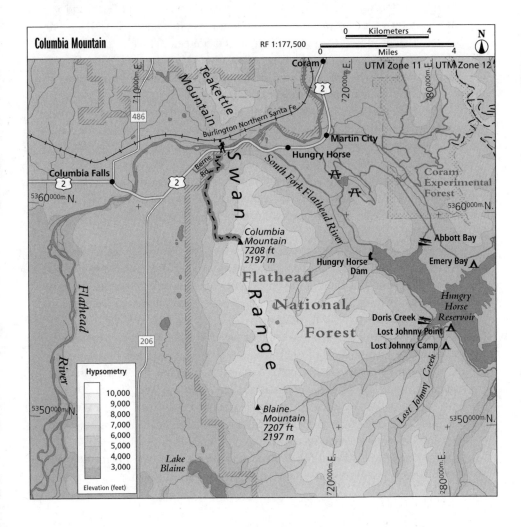

Jewel Basin, Gem of the Swan

Perhaps the only real challenge of venturing into Jewel Basin is the 8-mile drive from near Echo Lake to the parking lot near Noisy Basin. Yes, the road up is rough, but taken slowly it is navigable and well worth the effort. Views from the road only suggest the grandeur ahead.

From the parking lot it is about a forty-five-minute drive up a steep grade to the trailhead for Black Lake and the Picnic Lakes (to the north) and Birch and Crater Lakes (to the southeast). We chose the latter direction. Yet another hour and you can shed your packs and fish the sunlit waters of Birch Lake, located on the southern flank of Mount Aeneas.

Including the drive from Bigfork, the journey to Birch Lake usually takes about three hours. Along the entire route are panoramic views of Flathead Lake and the lower valley, as well as the Swan and Mission Mountains stretching to the south. The walk in to Birch Lake from the trailhead provides a mixture of uphill and downhill hiking, which is not overly tiring. The trail will take you through flower-filled meadows and glades along hillsides, offering views of rocky peaks, gushing streams, and waterfalls.

Jewel Basin lies east and slightly north of Bigfork and approximately 17 miles southeast of both Kalispell and Columbia Falls. "The Jewel" straddles the Swan Range within sight of Flathead Lake to the south and Hungry Horse Reservoir to the east. It's a hiker's and backpacker's dream and more than fulfills the promise the Forest Service envisioned when giving the area its special designation more than forty years ago. No logging or other resource extraction is permitted in the basin, and no horses, domestic livestock, or motorized vehicles are allowed.

When the Jewel Basin Hiking Area was created, the Forest Service envisioned an easily accessible trail transportation system conducive to short family hikes and offering people of all ages the opportunity to enjoy nature without the burden of expensive equipment or the need to possess great physical endurance. So far the area has discharged its duty well.

As planned, easy access is the region's premier asset. Roads approach close to the hiking area boundary in both the Noisy and Graves Creek drainages, on the west and east sides, respectively. In addition to Graves Creek, the northern and eastern portions of the area are accessible along the West Side South Fork Road parallel to Hungry Horse Reservoir via Wounded Buck Road, West Fork Clayton Creek and Clayton Creek Roads, and Wheeler Creek Road. Access may also be gained via Krause Creek Road near the northeast corner of Jewel Basin.

Noisy Creek Road is by far the most popular access, used by 80 percent of the recreationists entering the area, and is within the closest walking distance to a lake in Jewel Basin. As noted, the road is rough and rocky and is not suitable for trailers, but small trucks and cars should have no problem.

Once within the boundaries of Jewel Basin, the hiker has more than 15,000 acres of high-mountain backcountry at his or her disposal. The area is characterized by glacier-carved peaks and cirques, which surround valleys dotted with thirty alpine lakes. Thirty-five miles of trails connect most of the lakes, and aside from getting from the valley floor to the basin rim, most of the hiking is not strenuous. The elevation varies from 4,200 feet to 7,530 at the top of Mount Aeneas.

Mountain goats are commonly seen and inhabit the region along with elk, mule deer, and a few white-tailed deer. Black and grizzly bears and an occasional mountain lion are also known to live in the basin. You also may see such upland game birds as Franklin, blue, and ruffed grouse. Furbearing mammals in the region include pine martens, weasels, and coyotes. There is also a sparse population of lynx, minks, beavers, and badgers.

Fishing in the basin's lakes is quite good. Populations of westslope cutthroat trout are maintained in many of the lakes by Montana Fish, Wildlife and Parks through a planting program. Big Hawk, Birch, Black, Blackfoot, Wildcat, Pilgrim, Clayton, and Crater Lakes are cited most often as providing the best fishing.

All manner of baits and lures have proved effective. Shiny brass lures and red spinners are sometimes called for, as are cheese, marshmallows, and worms. Flies can be effective if the fish are rising near the shore—or if you are keen and long of cast with a fly rod. An enterprising and hardy soul might pack in a float tube and find success in the deeper center portions of the bigger lakes.

Lakes occupy 383 acres, about 2 percent of the land area, in Jewel Basin. Clayton Lake in the northeast corner supports a cutthroat trout population and, at fifty-eight acres, is the basin's largest body of water. At 100 feet, it is nearly the deepest. Next in size come Upper Black Lake, Wildcat Lake, and Birch Lake, which is close to the Noisy Basin access, providing excellent fishing with its population of rainbow and cutthroat trout and its 105-foot depth.

Interest in preserving the unique status of Jewel Basin began in the 1950s, and although the basin lost its bid to be established as a wilderness area, it was designated a hiking area soon after. As such, it is off-limits to horses, all forms of wheeled vehicles, and all forms of motorized vehicles, including snowmobiles.

Today the 15,349-acre Jewel Basin Hiking Area is a model of order and provision. All trailheads and intersections are marked with simple directional signs that also show the mileages to various lake and campground destinations.

Mount Aeneas

Although the Jewel Basin Hiking Area does not provide mountains that stagger the imagination by virtue of exceptional elevation, it does offer several mountains with great relief that tower above their surroundings. The tallest of these is Mount Aeneas (7,477 feet).

Big Knife, an Iroquois Indian, arrived in the Flathead sometime in the 1870s and was adopted by the Kootenai people. Somewhere along the way his name was changed to Aeneas, borrowed from the Greek, meaning "Man without a Country."

Elaine Snyder, a volunteer hike leader with the Montana Wilderness Association, says that from the top of Mount Aeneas you can see in several directions and that your sweep includes vistas of early Indian settlements, some thousands of years old. "There are places," says Snyder, "that were used in the last century by Native Americans who camped, hunted, and gathered in the valley." Snyder says that there is good evidence that the peak itself was an important perspective point for early-day hunters, just as it is for us.

According to Snyder, Bob Marshall once hiked the area, walking through what is now the Bob Marshall Wilderness in late August 1928. According to his trail diary, Marshall "...climbed to the summit of Mt. Aeneas at 11:10 A.M., [and paused] for seven minutes before heading down the pass." Although the climb to the summit was not challenging, Marshall also notes that on that particular

A mountain goat attracts hikers bound for Mount Aeneas, which looms in the background.

day he covered 30 miles—an impressive distance, particularly in the mountains forming the Swans.

On this hike you'll get unobstructed views of Big Mountain and the Flathead Valley. From the summit (after gaining 4,100 feet), you'll see into Glacier National Park to the north, the Great Bear Wilderness to the east, and the Swan Range to the south.

From the summit retrace your steps back down. If you're out for a trip of several days, take the right-hand trail (to the south) and follow it to Strawberry Mountain and then on into the Jewel Basin Hiking Area.

To reach the trailhead, take US 2 northeast from Columbia Falls, following the trailhead signs. Take a right onto Berne Road (off US 2) and follow it to the north end for the trailhead.

Yellow glacier lilies are one of the first flowers to emerge in spring.

Chapter 14
Cycling in the Flathead Valley

Cycling is one of the most popular sports in the area. Miles and miles of routes exist on which to ride, from extreme mountain biking to rides on the flats. Here we've listed a few places that are personal favorites. Access www.montanas flatheadvalley.com for trails and bike rentals.

Great Northern Historical Trail

The ultimate goal of the Rails-to-Trails of Northwest Montana is to have a path along the old Burlington Northern Railroad route from the turnoff to the town of Somers (at the north end of Flathead Lake) to the town of Marion, west of Kalispell. The following portions of the trail exist now:

1. Start from Meridian Road in Kalispell on U.S. Highway 2 West, or take Foys Lake Road west to Dern Road and begin there. The trail ends at Kila.
2. From Highway 82 at the turnoff to the town of Somers at the north end of Flathead Lake, the bike path goes north, paralleling U.S. Highway 93 toward Kalispell for 6 miles to Ashley Creek.

Columbia Falls

This moderate 23-mile out-and-back road ride on the North Fork Road (County Road 486) is accessed from Nucleus Avenue in Columbia Falls. You'll ride along forestlands to the west and the Wild and Scenic North Fork of the Flathead River to the east along the border of Glacier National Park.

Big Mountain Coast

An 8-mile mountain bike descent from the top of Big Mountain Ski Resort in Whitefish, this trek is rated a moderate mountain bike trail. It's all downhill (check your brakes), since you can ride the Glacier Chaser gondola to the top, high into the Rockies. When you get there, the views of Glacier National Park and surrounding valleys are incredible. Then it's 8 miles downhill.

To reach the resort, take US 93 north to the right-hand, signed turn to Big Mountain.

Star Meadow

A moderate 36-mile road-bike ride, this is a favorite; there is little traffic on the road. But it isn't all flat; there are some good hills here as you wind by creeks, meadows, and ranches. In addition, there are good opportunities to spot wildlife.

You'll begin at the Round Meadow Ski Area and travel west to Star Meadow Ranch (14 miles from Round Meadow). If you want to explore only the Round Meadow area by bike, you can ride the cross-country ski loops here; just follow the blazed ski trail signs.

To reach Round Meadow Ski Area, travel north on US 93 from Whitefish for 11 miles to the left-hand turn onto Farm-to-Market Road (there will be a sign for Round Meadow at the turn). Go 2 miles; turn right onto Star Meadow Road and travel 2 miles to the Round Meadow parking area.

Tally Lake Area

The Tally Lake area, to the west of Whitefish, offers miles of bike routes, from 0.5 mile to 20 miles. Plan to camp at the Forest Service campground at Tally Lake and strike out from there to wherever suits your fancy.

To reach Tally Lake, take US 93 north out of Kalispell toward Whitefish. Turn left onto West Reserve Drive at a four-way stop just beyond the mall area; go 4 miles to Farm-to-Market Road and turn right. Go 9 miles to Tally Lake Road and the campground on your left. Turn left and follow the road to the campground.

In spring 2004, Ruth Barber of Somers, Montana, hauled in a record lake trout from Flathead Lake. The fish weighed 42 pounds 11.8 ounces and spanned 42.5 inches. With its deeply forked tail, light spots set against a dark background, and a girth of 31 inches, the fish was indeed a beautiful specimen.

Although fish of those dimensions are unusual, it is not uncommon in the Flathead Lake to pull out a lake trout that might weigh 5 to 10 pounds and span 24 inches, something I have often done. That is not to say anglers won't haul in yet another record fish. The lake contains—as one man likes to say—"a plethora of piscine prizes," adding, "you never know when you're going to land one!"

Fishing Flathead Lake and its three main drainages can be challenging. In addition to being the largest freshwater lake west of the Mississippi, the lake's three main tributaries also claim superlative status. They drain Glacier National Park as well as the Great Bear and Bob Marshall Wildernesses. But let's segment these hundreds of miles of fishable waters, beginning with huge Flathead Lake, prefacing it all by saying that if you've got ten days to two weeks, you can literally fish your way through the Flathead.

Although experienced anglers consistently catch fish in 27-by-15-mile Flathead Lake, newcomers should seek assistance. George "Shorty" Goggins has been guiding clients from a craft of his own design for a quarter of a century, and joining the man for a day is instructive—he knows the hot spots, and he knows how to fish them.

Although Flathead offers other large species, the lake trout (or mackinaw) is the biggest denizen of these deep waters, which in spots sink 370 feet. The waters are clear and tantalizing, but generally you'll want to extend your line no more than 30 to 100 feet. As is the case with many other fish species, early morning and late evening are best, and that's especially true of lake trout, which prefer dim light.

Perhaps one of the biggest advantages of fishing Flathead Lake is that it is surrounded by Flathead Lake State Park. The park is divided into seven different units, and each offers various forms of camping. A popular campground is located at Big Arm, where many of the sites are immediately adjacent to the water. If you have a kayak and are camped there, you are truly blessed. You can paddle to nearby Wild Horse Island, where fishing the coves and shore can sometimes be productive. If you take time to beach your kayak and hike the

"Shorty" Goggins runs a successful charter service on Flathead Lake.

island, I guarantee that you'll see huge deer and beautiful bands of bighorn sheep.

Flathead Lake provides an excellent fishery, but its size can sometimes overwhelm, particularly if you don't have a boat. Don't be discouraged; many other options exist. Over the years, the State of Montana has purchased easements that enable fishermen to easily access the Flathead all along the lakeshore and its tributaries. As a result, fishermen have access to about a dozen sites. Montana Fish, Wildlife and Parks has produced a pamphlet called *Access Sites;* and you should obtain a copy. If you decide to fish the tributaries, you've made another good decision, but you still must pay homage to Flathead Lake.

In FalconGuides' *Fishing Montana* (The Globe Pequot Press), Michael Sample says that anglers have the lake to thank for providing quarry on a seasonal basis. "The lake acts like a giant heart, pumping pulses of fish into its arteries. In spring, cutthroat and bull trout start their spawning runs; in fall, major pulses of mountain whitefish follow." In other words, what you catch depends on the season you're here.

If you're here in the spring and look over the bridge on Highway 35 just before reaching Kalispell from the east, you'll see dozens of fishermen lining the banks of the Flathead River. In fact, that's what they're doing all along the river at access sites from the bridge to the river's mouth.

In part they're catching the spring run of cutthroat, but they're also after lake trout, which feed on local populations of whitefish. Be aware that you've got a mixture of bull trout thrown in. Because the species is threatened, you must be able to identify it so that you can release it.

Because identifying bull trout can be tricky, state information and education officer John Fraley has a suggestion. He says you can generally look to the dorsal fin to differentiate between lake and bull trout, relying on a simple rhyme: "If you don't see black, put it back."

That's the way it is in spring. But fast-forward now to autumn. Again, look from the Highway 35 bridge, but this time you'll see anglers along the shores or sitting in boats braving the cold. Look again and you'll see a dedicated soul fishing from a large johnboat, wearing dark Malone wool trousers and a down parka with hood pulled tight. That's me, and I'm after mountain whitefish—a wonderful prize. I smoke them in an old refrigerator using apple wood and my own secret brine.

Now we're down to summer, and if you want to remain in Flathead River proper, you'll want to concentrate on pike. If you are willing to rent a canoe, you can access Egan Slough from Highway 35 just about 5 miles east of the bridge by taking the Montford Road south. There you'll have to ask permission to cross private property, which is usually given. Egan Slough provides a respectable pike fishery; I have taken pike here that weighed well over 5 pounds. If you have a riverworthy boat, you can access Church, Fennon, and Half Moon Sloughs from the river. But if you're into trout, you need to look north to the tributaries. And if you're into remote waters, you'll want to try the South Fork of the Flathead, with its huge reservoir. From tiny Hungry Horse, Montana, you can access Hungry Horse Reservoir from literally dozens of primitive Forest Service campgrounds with names like Lost Johnny, Lake View, and Devils Corkscrew. You can fish these areas from the shore, but if you have some type of watercraft, you're in even better shape.

If these areas aren't remote enough, continue driving the gravel road above the reservoir to Meadow Creek trailhead. Check your map for trails leading to the river between the reservoir and the Meadow Creek trailhead. Either fish the shores or launch a raft, and then begin angling for westslope cutthroat trout.

Westslope cutthroat is another species that has been influenced by man. About the turn of the twentieth century, newcomers who wanted to improve the fishery introduced rainbow trout. In places the two species have formed a hybrid known as "cutbow." You may catch one or two of the hybrids, but the pure westslope version has a bright red mark along the lower jaw that boldly proclaims it to be cutthroat.

Regardless of the hybrid fiasco, the South Fork above Hungry Horse Reservoir can provide some incredible catches. Jim Vashro of Montana's Fish, Wildlife and Parks says the South Fork is incredible and that cutthroat range from 400 to 1,000 fish per mile. However, for cutthroat, the South Fork, along with the entire Flathead River drainage, is now catch-and-release.

Although you can also fish the Middle Fork, which creates a boundary to Glacier National Park's eastern flanks, I've never had much luck there. I prefer the North Fork, and it has as much to do with the fact that this tributary forms a remote western boundary of the park as it does with the quality of fishing, which can be excellent. I worked at the national park during my college years, and I remember several occasions when I was fishing a quiet pool on the North Fork and saw deer and grouse. On more than one occasion I saw grizzly bears.

The first quarter of the North Fork pours out of Canada to the little outpost called Polebridge. If you have a raft, this entire 59-mile section down to the North Fork's confluence with the Middle Fork provides a wonderful float and some first-class fishing. My suggestion is to select a short segment and then work the pools and riffles for trout.

In many places the river can also be accessed by car. There are many opportunities to park along this gravel road, and you may want to try a number of spots. There are also campgrounds with river access; check your map. We like the one at Big Creek. Pitch your tent and then take day drives.

I am both a fly fisherman and a spin caster, and if I really want to catch a fish, I'm prone to rely on red-and-white Daredevils or perhaps a gold-colored

Mepps. But if I want to elevate the concept of *fishing* to the concept of *angling*, I use flies—specifically the Royal Coachman, Elk Hair Caddis, Wulffs, Humpies, and perhaps Joe's Hoppers. When casting a Coachman into waters just behind a riffle, more than once I've pulled out a large cutthroat. And once, using a dragonfly nymph and jerking it along the bottom, I pulled out a large westslope cutthroat. Although it wasn't a trophy, it was nevertheless a beautiful specimen. I took a moment to admire the long slash mark along its jaw and the dark spots, which began near the mouth and then increased in density as they continued onto the tail. This is the same species Lewis and Clark had so admired, and I quickly released it, thinking that I might catch it again next year, but as an even larger specimen. Fish of this type grow to lengths of 18 inches and sometimes weigh 2 to 3 pounds. The species could again become common, delighting us all as a true piscine prize.

That's the hope and that's the allure, for just like Ruth Barber and her lunker lake trout, you never know when you're going to catch one.

Trees bend to the weight of ice and snow when moisture-laden clouds form snow ghosts.

Ten Days in the Bob

When a bull elk passes through your camp only hours before hunting season opens—bugling and snorting for all it's worth—that is a significant sign.

Some may consider such an event to carry ominous overtones, but that was not the feeling of those in our camp. Within seconds the camp was alive with chatter, although the stars were still out and dawn was a full five hours away.

Our group was a commercial hunting party, and we were about 16 miles from the nearest road, camped near Big Salmon Lake in the Bob Marshall Wilderness (the "Bob"). Unless you own a horse, the services provided by a professional outfitter are essential if you want to bag an elk. Backpackers have little chance of sectioning an 800-pound elk and packing it out before the carcass begins to deteriorate. As a result, more and more hunters are relying on commercial outfitters.

In the Bob Marshall Wilderness, the Forest Service issues outfitters a permit and then specifies where they must locate the base camp. In the Bob, about thirty permits are issued to registered guides. Each guide must then file an itinerary and list the number of people going on each outing.

Guided trips essentially come in two packages. One, the drop camp, gets hunters into an area of their choosing. Clients are dropped off and then picked up after a specified length of time.

Our group's trip was the second type and came with all the trimmings: Meals were cooked, guide service provided, and game packed out immediately. Our group included hunters from California, Montana, and Nevada.

Horses and mules carried our gear, and this group included several unbroken horses our outfitter had acquired from a wild Nevada herd under the Adopt-a-Horse program. The horses are actually given away—the only stipulation is that they cannot be used as commercial riding horses for one year. Never broken, the horses virtually had to be hog-tied before a saddle could be applied. Surprisingly each horse quickly adapted to both saddle and load. As part of the string, they were placed between trail-wise animals.

Sixteen miles and four and a half hours later, base camp looked pretty good. The oldest member of our party, a sixty-seven-year-old man from California, dismounted and walked part of the way. Spry as could be, the man had just not ridden much in recent months.

An elk hunting trip deep into the Bob Marshall Wilderness was reached by pack trip.

On the first morning of the hunt, camp was alive several hours before dawn. Plans were made based on the experience our outfitter had acquired from hunting in the Bob and bagging an elk every year for more than twenty years. It was decided that I would go up Dart Creek, which was fine with me. I was sure the bugling bull had headed in that direction.

By sunrise I was in a tangle of snowbrush. The vegetation was so thick that we had to crawl much of the time. Still, elk wallows were everywhere, and the scent of rutting elk was strong. But the brush was dry—too dry—and I decided to climb high, where the noise would not announce my every movement.

By noon I was near the top of a ridge and although sign was still abundant, the only animals I saw were goats grazing off in the distance. Half an hour later I heard the crack of another hunter's rifle, followed almost immediately by another crack, then a pause, and another shot. I sat down, thinking the elk might be wounded and maybe moving in my direction. Then I heard the hunter's excited holler, a holler to hurry.

He had bagged a beautiful six-point bull elk—a royal that we guessed weighed about 800 pounds. The day was hot, so we quickly dressed out the elk, elevated it over a makeshift frame of logs, and covered it with boughs. The carcass was already cooling, and before we left the guide extracted the elk's teeth.

Bagging an elk is one thing; getting it out is another. Leaving early next morning, five of us spent the better part of a fourteen-hour day wrangling mules through brush and up incredibly steep terrain. Back at base camp that night, the cold beer packed in by the mules tasted mighty good.

Early the next day, the quartered elk was packed out to Condon, Montana, for storage.

No more elk were taken on that trip or even heard bugling until the day I was leaving. The bull chose the middle of the day to herald his presence, which was encouraging for me—I had been invited for yet another hunt later in the fall.

Boone and Crockett Records

The Boone & Crockett Scores in the following table show how the Flathead measures up in hunting throughout the state. Regarding the whitetail, Jim Williams of Montana Fish, Wildlife and Parks (MFW) says that if Kent Petry's number-two deer had been measured sooner (before antler shrinkage) his deer might hold the number-one record. So if you are a trophy hunter, or a person simply interested in knowing how well the Flathead rates, here's your guide to put you in the know.

Species	Montana Number-One Ranking	Flathead Ranking	Hunter (in Flathead)
Black Bear	21 8/16 Fergus County	20 14/16 (1986) 7th	Workman, Victor
Grizzly Bear	25 9/16 (1890) Missouri Breaks	23 14/16 (1965) 9th	Weiss, Bruno
Mountain Lion		15 13/16 (1985) 1st	Bell, Jeff
American Elk	419 4/8 (1958) Madison County	386 6/8 (1976) 23rd	Jackson, Floyd L.
Mule Deer	205 3/8 (1983) Custer County	197 2/8 (1986) 9th	Vetter, Jim
White-tailed Deer	199 3/8 (1974) Missoula County	199 2/8 (1966) 2nd	Petry, Kent M.
		191 5/8 (1963) 3rd	McMaster, Earl
Moose	195 1/8 (1952) Red Rock Lakes	179 6/8 (1988) 9th	Clanton, Mike
Goat		54 0/8 (1998) 1st	Beatty, Jason D.

Chapter 17
Winter Sports

Winter sports are extremely popular throughout the Flathead Valley, helping prevent "cabin fever." So get a map detailing your sport (available at most stores and at the Flathead Convention and Visitor Bureau in Kalispell), pull on the fleece, and pray for snow!

Cross-Country Skiing and Snowshoeing

When snow covers the valley, winter enthusiasts have a multitude of places from which to choose. From high up on a mountain trail to cross-country courses on the valley floor, there's a place for everyone. Remember, particularly if you are venturing into the backcountry for any winter sports, that northwestern Montana has its share of avalanches. Be sure to carry the proper avalanche equipment (probe, beacon, and shovel), survival gear, extra food, and extra clothing. When avalanche danger is high, warnings are posted in the newspapers and on the radio. Call the administering bodies of the area you'll be visiting for updates before starting out. When in doubt, don't venture out.

High Trails

Izaak Walton Inn

The Izaak Walton Inn in Essex (bordering Glacier National Park) offers about 20.5 miles of groomed trails for beginner through advanced skiers. A short (1 kilometer/0.6 mile) part of the Starlight Trail is lighted at night for skiers. You don't even have to worry about getting stuck up here in a blizzard—the inn offers rooms and great meals! (Call ahead at busy times.) There is a trail fee for day users; lessons are available; skis and snowshoes can be rented. The inn can provide guides for ski tours into Glacier National Park. Several types of ski races are held during December, January, and March.

Take U.S. Highway 2 east from West Glacier for about 37 miles to the sign for the inn on your right. Call the inn at (406) 888–5700 for information.

Big Mountain Nordic Center

Big Mountain Nordic Center offers 9.9 miles of groomed ski trails, usable for both skate-skiing and traditional Nordic skiing. You'll also find snowshoe trails here. The entrance to the center is adjacent to the Outpost Lodge at the bottom of chair 6; trail maps, lessons, tours, and rentals are available for a fee. Those possessing season ski tickets may use the cross-country course at no additional charge. Call (406) 862–2900 for information.

Blacktail Mountain Area

Flathead County administers the free cross-country trails in the Blacktail area at the south end of Lakeside on the west side of Flathead Lake. There are four ski loops from 5.25 to 8 miles, ranging from easy to difficult. The trails are usually groomed once a week.

Heading south on US 93 from Lakeside, take the signed (TO BLACKTAIL MT) road on the right (west) at the end of town. There will be signs for the two parking lots for the loops. The lower parking area, at Mile 6.4, holds five cars; the upper, at Mile 8.1, holds ten cars. The upper lot is the better area to start from; you can access all four trails from here. It is advisable to have chains or studded snow tires on your vehicle, although the road is usually plowed because Blacktail ski slope (at the top) users also travel this road. Call the Parks and Recreation Department at (406) 758–5800 for information. Some local shops in Lakeside may have trail maps available.

Valley Trails

Glacier Nordic Center

The Whitefish Lake Golf Course, located at 1200 U.S. Highway 93 North, offers 7.4 miles of trails, with 1.8 miles lighted for night skiing. Children under twelve ski free; there is a small charge for adults. Season passes are also available. The Outback Ski Shack near the pro shop offers lessons and rentals.

For further information call (406) 862–9498.

Round Meadows

If you don't mind traveling 13 miles northwest of Whitefish, try Round Meadows, with 10 miles of trails for skiers. Beginner and expert skiers will enjoy the trails that range from gentle hills to difficult ones.

Take US 93 northwest out of Whitefish for 10.2 miles. Turn left on Farm-to-Market Road and go 2 miles. Turn right on Star Meadows Road (County Road 539) and go 1 mile to the parking lot on your right. Maps are available at the trailhead. For trail conditions call (406) 863–5420 or the Tally Lake Ranger District at (406) 863–5400 for information.

Stillwater Mountain Lodge

If you want to see beautiful views and to be close to nature in the forests, on ridges, and by lakes, try Stillwater Mountain Lodge, a place developed by three families for the community to enjoy. You can even take your pooch on 3.5 kilometers of the 20-kilometer trail system, much of which is a system of loops. Trails are groomed for skate skiing, with tracks for classic skiing.

Annual or daily ski passes are available, with daily prices ranging from $6.00 to $8.00. All skiers, including guests, must purchase a Montana State Land Use Permit ($7.00); a valid Montana hunting/fishing license will suffice for the Land Use Permit. And imagine this: According to local papers, the owners say that if you can't afford a ski pass, you can work off the cost by doing trail work!

The restored lodge, which can hold up to fourteen people, and the trails are located 8 miles northwest of Whitefish at 750 Beaver Lake Road. Take US 93 north out of Whitefish for 7 miles until you see the brown sign for Beaver Lake fishing access; turn right onto Beaver Lake Road. Stay right at the Y and go 1.5 miles to the lodge on your left. For information call (406) 862–7004 or visit www.stillwatermtnlodge.com.

Meadow Lake

The Meadow Lake Golf Course in Columbia Falls offers free skiing. Stop at the North Fork Grill at the golf course for maps and information, or call (406) 892–8700.

Bigfork Nordic Center

Located in the foothills beneath the Jewel Basin area of the Swan Range, the Nordic Center has approximately 6 miles of trails winding through the Flathead National Forest. Log on at www.bigforknordic.org for information. Some years a forest recreation permit is required, available at gas stations and sporting good shops.

To get to this fun, family-oriented trail system, take Highway 35 north from Bigfork to Highway 83. Go east on Highway 83 to Echo Lake Road. Turn left (north) onto Echo Lake Road and follow the signs for Jewel Basin. As you turn right (east) on the Jewel Basin Road, you'll see a small parking area on the right. The trails begin on the left.

Swan Mountain Ranch

If you're looking for a place that's a bit more remote, try the Swan Mountain Ranch, located about 7 miles south of Swan Lake. The ranch has 18.6 miles of groomed trails and an ice-skating pond and offers meals and lodging (a main lodge and a guest cabin). A fee is charged for daily use, but those under six and over seventy go free. Nice dogs are allowed. To get to Swan Lake, take Highway 83 south, which is located just north of Bigfork on Highway 35 north. Call (406) 886–3900 for information.

For more cross-country trails in this area, try the Laughing Horse Lodge in Swan Lake, with a hotel and 50 miles of ungroomed backcountry trails (call 406–886–2080). Nice dogs are allowed here, too. Another fun place is the Swan

Lake Wildlife Refuge, just south of the town of Swan Lake. The refuge has three 3.7-mile loops of backcountry skiing.

Kalispell

Herron Park

Herron Park, 5 miles west of Kalispell on Foys Lake Road, has 7 miles of ski trails geared to all levels of skiers. There is no charge, and trails are groomed periodically. Call Flathead County Parks and Recreation at (406) 758–5800 for maps and information.

Buffalo Hill Golf Course

Buffalo Hill Golf Course is open for free skiing on its twenty-seven holes, which are groomed by volunteers. This course is for classic skiers and doesn't have enough snow to groom for skate-skiers. Beginners to intermediates will enjoy this course and can buy food while warming up in the clubhouse. Call (406) 756–4545 for information. The course is located off US 93 behind the Kalispell Regional Medical Center, along the Stillwater River near Whitefish Stage. Dogs are not allowed, and only skiers should use the groomed trails.

Downhill Skiing and Snowboarding

Big Mountain (www.bigmtn.com), soaring above the town of Whitefish, has long been a draw for skiers, both expert and novice. The complex seems to expand annually, with something new and different being offered each year.

With a summit elevation of 6,817 feet and a vertical drop of 2,353 feet, Big Mountain is a challenge. But there is something here for the beginner right up to the expert. There are thirteen lifts servicing the 3,000 acres; the longest run, Hellfire, is 3.3 miles.

Recently the resort added a new superpipe, a terrain park, and a "magic carpet ride" lift for beginners. Snowboarders take note: The superpipe is 450 feet long, 65 feet wide, and 15 feet high.

Big Mountain offers a bit of everything, from restaurants (ten) to bars, rental facilities, spas, stores, and lots of lodging. In 2005 the daily lift fees ranged from $39 for seniors and students to $49 for adults. If you're over eighty or under six, you go for free! The season ends around the beginning of April with only one trail open, in part to protect grizzly bears coming out of hibernation that roam these mountains during stressful times.

To get to Big Mountain, follow US 93 north from Kalispell to the four-way intersection where US 93 goes left to Eureka. Cross the intersection, getting on Wisconsin Avenue. Follow that to Big Mountain Road on the right. Then it's about 5 miles up to the top. Or take a free shuttle from Whitefish; call (406)

On Big Mountain skiers stop to marvel at the buildup of snow ghosts.

862–1900 for schedule information. For snow reports call the snow phone: (406) 862–7669; for general information call (406) 862–1900.

Blacktail Mountain Ski Area (www.black-tailmountain.com) began its ninth year in 2006. It came into existence because of the need and desire for an affordable ski area geared toward families. *Ski Magazine* called Blacktail "the quintessential local resort."

The mountain has a vertical drop of 1,440 feet, twenty-four runs, three lifts plus a rope tow, and 1,170 acres to ski on, including 70 acres of tree skiing. Lift tickets are $22 for college students, $30 for adults, and $20 for teens; those over seventy or under seven ski free. Half-day rates are offered after 1:00 P.M. At the top, where everything begins, is a 17,000-square-foot lodge where all your needs (rentals, lessons, food, and drink) are met.

Blacktail is open Wednesday through Sunday, and seven days a week during the Christmas holidays. For general information call (406) 844–0999.

The road to Blacktail Mountain is located at the southern end of the town of Lakeside on US 93 (south of Kalispell). The signs for turning west onto Blacktail Mountain Road are clearly visible. Or take advantage of the $5.00 round-trip shuttle (the Blacktail Express) that comes and goes daily from Kalispell, Somers, and Lakeside (also from Bigfork on weekends only). For stop locations, times, and reservations, call (406) 844–0808.

Ice Skating

The Flathead Valley boasts two ice-skating rinks, with a third at the Izaak Walton Inn in Essex.

The Stumptown Ice Den in Whitefish is very popular and is managed by the Whitefish Parks and Recreation Department. The area has a roof and is walled on two sides. It offers night lighting, a lobby, rentals, and a food stand. Fees for daily skating are $4.50; skate rentals are $2.25. There is a small charge for group lessons. The Den offers much more, including hockey and special tournaments. It's important to call for information (406–863–2477), as the rink has a lot going on each day. The rink is located at 725½ Wisconsin Avenue on the way to Big Mountain.

Woodland Park in Kalispell is another popular outdoor skating spot. You can skate free from 10:00 A.M. to 11:00 P.M. (it's lighted at night) each day, provided the ice is safe. Children can get lessons for a nominal fee; these usually begin around Christmas. Call (406) 758–5800 for information.

The Izaak Walton Inn in Essex has a 40-by-60-foot outdoor rink, with a pavilion-style roof and lighting. You can use the rink day and evening. The daily fee is $5.00, unless you are a guest; rentals are also $5.00. Call (406) 888–5700 for information. The inn is located on US 2, about 37 miles east of West Glacier.

Snowmobiling

Because northwest Montana is such a popular snowmobile destination, there are a few things you might want to know. Nonresidents will need a snowmobile permit, about $15 per machine. Permits are available from Montana Fish, Wildlife and Parks and from snowmobile retailers, hotels, and motels.

Additionally, you'll need a public land permit, and machines must be registered with current decals from the Montana county in which the owner resides. If you ride on state land, you're also required to purchase a state-use permit, available at Fish, Wildlife and Parks. MFW will also furnish copies of laws pertaining to snowmobile use.

Avalanche-prone slopes pose danger, and you should be aware of the risks. Forest Service courses are often available. Always carry a probe, beacon, and shovel. You can access the Web site at www.avalanche-center.org or call (406) 587–6981 for up-to-date information. The Glacier Country Avalanche Center can be reached at (406) 257–8204.

Where to Go

There are more than 200 miles of groomed snowmobile trails in northwest Montana connecting from the North Fork of the Flathead River to Big Mountain in Whitefish to upper Whitefish Lake. Most trails are usually groomed weekly by the Flathead Snowmobiling Association. J and L Rentals at 5410 US 2 West in Columbia Falls (406–892–7666) is the only outfitter licensed to guide on USDA Forest Service land in northwest Montana. They also can provide you with avalanche emergency gear. Many other outfits in the valley also rent snowmobiles. Check the Yellow Pages for listings. You can also contact the Flathead Convention and Visitor Bureau for information at (406) 756–9091.

Following are some of the most scenic and popular destinations.

- **Whitefish Range:** Stryker Ridge and Werner Peak overlook areas
- **South Fork of the Flathead River:** Desert Mountain
- **Big Mountain:** summit
- **North Fork of the Flathead:** Kimmerly Basin, off the Canyon Creek Road
- **West side of Hungry Horse Reservoir** (the South Fork): a popular backcountry destination
- **South of Kalispell on Highway 83:** Seeley-Swan Valley.

Recently the Flathead National Forest set restrictions for snowmobiling on forestland in northwest Montana. Some large remote areas of land are now closed. Accessible areas offer ways into the groomed trails and "play areas."

Snowmobiling in the Swan Mountains of the Flathead Valley.

To know where you can and cannot go, pick up the winter recreation maps available at Forest Service offices. In Kalispell the office is located at 1935 Third Avenue East (406–758–5204). Ranger stations are located in Bigfork (406–837–7544) and in Hungry Horse at 8975 US 2 East (406–387–3800).

Dogsledding

The valley is not just for fair-weather enthusiasts. Dogsledding is a treat, a sport that gets you out into the silent woods, pulled along by a bunch of dogs that are crazy about their job. Anyone can participate, from grandparents to small children.

Jeff Ulsamer is a musher who operates Dog Sled Adventures from his home in Olney, 18 miles northwest of Whitefish on US 93 North. Ulsamer has been mushing for twenty-odd years now, and his love of the sport and of his dogs is apparent. He usually offers three sled runs a day, with three sleds as the maximum. Between eighty and ninety dogs make their home with Ulsamer, which allows him to use fresh dogs constantly. The trip goes along a 12-mile trail through the Stillwater National Forest, surrounded by such places as Dog Creek, Dog Lake, and Dog Mountain.

Ulsamer looks like a Montana mountain man, but gruff he is not. Along the trail he speaks his commands softly to his team—and the dogs respond easily, some with near grins on their faces. You may see wolf tracks or even a wolf along the trail, as well as elk and deer.

Imagine being tucked into a large padded sled, bundled all around with warm elk hides, gliding through a gentle forest as soft snow falls. To top it off, you'll be drinking hot chocolate and eating homemade cookies back in the lodge at trip's end. Perhaps Ulsamer will even treat you to some not-so-tall tales, if he's not too busy. Outside, the dogs are howling as they wait for another bunch of dog lovers to arrive to take a trip. Sound romantic as well as fun? You bet.

When the winter doldrums set in and the valley is blanketed in snow, try a little dogsledding. Trips with Dog Sled Adventures begin in December and run through March. Call (406) 881-2275 for information and reservations.

Big Mountain Ski Resort also offers dogsledding, also by Dog Sled Adventures, for a half-hour tour in the woods on Big Mountain. The sleds go on Tuesday and Thursday in the afternoon. Adults are $75; children twelve and under are $35. Call (406) 862-2900 for information and reservations.

Jeff Ulsamer runs Dog Sled Adventures for exploring the heart of the winter woods in Stillwater National Forest.

Glacier National Park: Park Headquarters, P.O. Box 128, West Glacier, MT 59936. Log on to www.nps.gov/glac/. For general information call (406) 888–7800; for boat tours call (406) 257–2426; for horseback riding call (406) 732–4203. Red Bus tours, call (406) 892–2525; Blackfeet Culture Sun Tours, (406) 226–9220 or (800) SUN–9220. For camping reservations at Fish Creek and St. Mary campgrounds, call (800) 365–CAMP (2267).

The park has three visitor centers: Apgar, on the west side of the park, in Apgar Village; Logan Pass Visitor Center, at the summit of Going-to-the-Sun Road; and St. Mary Visitor Center, on the east side of the park at the eastern terminus of Going-to-the-Sun Road.

Glacier Natural History Association: (406) 888–5756; www.glacierassociation.org

The Glacier Institute: (406) 755–1211; www.glacierinstitute.org

Chambers of Commerce

Bigfork	(406) 837–5888
Columbia Falls	(406) 892–2072
Kalispell	(406) 758–2800
Lakeside/Somers	(406) 844–3715
Polson	(406) 883–5969
Whitefish	(406) 862–3501

Flathead Convention and Visitor Bureau: 15 Depot Park, Kalispell; (406) 756–9091, (800) 543–3105; e-mail: fcvb@fcvb.org. They have information on where to stay, where to eat, what to do, and where to go. Sporting goods stores may be able to provide you with the names of reputable guides for all-season sports and can also provide you with a map of your area of interest.

Wild Horse Island State Park: For information about the park or the Flathead Lake Park System and the five state-operated campgrounds, call (406) 752–5501.

Montana Fish, Wildlife and Parks (FWP): For fishing and boating regulations and for a brochure on Montana's Fishing Access Sites and the Flathead Lake Marine Trail, call (406) 752–5501 or write to 490 North Meridian Road, Kalispell, MT 59901.

Canoe/kayak rentals and instruction: Silver Moon Kayak Company, 1215 North Somers Road, Kalispell; (406) 752–3794; www.SilverMoon Kayak .com. Contact Bob Danford or Susan Conrad for kayak lessons. And do check out their great guided Kayak Moonlight Paddle trips, where you'll visit islands on Flathead Lake and enjoy some refreshments. For instructions and trips, contact Bobbi Gilmore at Glacier Sea Kayaking, 862–9010. Bobbi offers great lessons and has myriad guided trips planned for each year.

Flathead River maps ($2.00): Flathead Basin Commission, 109 Cooperative Way, Suite 110, Kalispell, MT 59901; (406) 752–0081

Big Mountain in Whitefish: For winter and summer activities call (800) 858–4152; for activities and events call (406) 862–2900.

Flathead County Parks and Recreation: Call (406) 758–5800.

National Forest information: Flathead National Forest, 1935 Third Avenue East, Kalispell; (406) 758–5200; www.fs.fed.us/r1/flathead/. Bitterroot National Forest, (406) 363–3131. Kootenai National Forest, 506 U.S. Highway 2 West, Libby, MT 59923; (406) 293–6211

Guide outfits are scattered throughout the valley; following is just a sampling:

Fishing with Shorty, (800) 231–5214 or (406) 257–5214

A Able Fishing & Tours, Kalispell; (406) 257–5214

Glacier Fishing Charters, Columbia Falls; (406) 892–2377

Great Northern Whitewater Resort, West Glacier; (406) 387–5340

Lion Creek Outfitters, Kalispell; (406) 755–3723

Montana River Anglers, Whitefish; (406) 862–3448

Northern Rockies Outfitters, Ltd., Kalispell; (406) 756–2544

Wild River Adventures, West Glacier; (406) 387–9453

Flathead Raft Company, Polson; (406) 883–5838

Glacier Raft Company, West Glacier; (406) 888–5454

Glacier Wilderness Guides/Montana Raft Company, West Glacier; (406) 387–5555 or (800) 521–7238

Silver Moon Kayak Co., Kalispell; (406) 752–3794

The Blackfeet Nation: P.O. Box 850, Browning, MT 59417; (406) 338–7276

The Confederated Salish and Kootenai Tribes: 51383 U.S. Highway 93 North, Pablo, MT; (406) 675–2700 or (888) 835–8766

Far West Cruises: (406) 857–3203

Flathead-Kootenai Chapter of Montana Wilderness Association: For both winter and summer guided hikes: (406) 755–6304

Glacier Park Boat Co.: (406) 257–2426

Pointer Scenic Cruises: (406) 837–5617

Questa Sailing Charters: (406) 837–5569

Stumptown Anglers: (406) 862–4554

Appendix B
Glacier National Park Campgrounds

The following campgrounds are operated on a first-come, first-served basis, except where noted.

Apgar—Open mid-May to mid-October; 194 sites. Open for primitive winter camping.

Avalanche—Open early June to learly September; 87 sites, with a 26-foot maximum RV length.

Bowman Lake—Open mid-May to mid-September; 48 sites; RVs not recommended. Bowman is accessed by a sometimes rough dirt road.

Cut Bank—This is a small campground; very short campers (18 feet). RVs not recommended. No potable water; primitive status all year.

Fish Creek—Open early June to early September; 180 sites, with a 27-foot maximum RV length. Reservations are on a first-apply basis: www.reservations .nps.gov; (800) 365–2267.

Kintla Lake—Open mid-May to mid-September; 13 sites, with a maximum trailer length of 18 feet. RVs not recommended. The road to Kintla is a dirt road.

Logging Creek—Located on the west side of the park on the rough, dirt Inside North Fork Road. RVs and trailers are not recommended due to road conditions. Open early July until early September; 8 sites, pit toilets, and a water pump. No potable water; primitive status year-round.

Many Glacier—Open late May to late September; 110 sites, with a maximum RV length of 35 feet.

Quartz Creek—This is a primitive campground on the park's west side on the Inside North Fork Road, a rough dirt road. RVs and trailers are not recommended due to road conditions. Open early July through early September; 7 sites, with pit toilets and a water pump. No potable water; primitive status year-round.

Rising Sun—Open late May to late September; 83 sites, with a maximum RV length of 25 feet.

Sprague Creek—Open mid-May to late September, the campground is located on the northeast shore of Lake McDonald, about 9 miles from the park's west entrance. There are 25 sites; no towed units are allowed due to road conditions. The campground has flush toilets, sinks, and running water.

St. Mary—Open late May to late September; 148 sites, with a maximum RV length of 35 feet. Reservations are on a first-apply basis: www.reservations. nps.gov; (800) 365–2267.

Two Medicine—Open late May to early September; 99 sites, with a maximum RV length of 32 feet.

Apgar, Bowman Lake, Kintla, Many Glacier, and Rising Sun have boat access; motors are prohibited at Kintla Lake and Many Glacier.

NOTE: The open-close dates for these campgrounds vary, depending on the weather. If there is no early snow, many campgrounds stay open later in the fall.

Appendix C
Glacier National Park Information

Fees

At this time entry fees range from $12 per individual (foot, bike, or motorcycle) to $25 per car, both valid for seven days. Glacier National Park and the National Parks passes are good for one year and cost $30 and $50, respectively. Waterton Lakes National Park in Canada has separate fees. There are no fees or licenses required to fish the streams and lakes of the park.

Vehicle Size Restrictions

If you plan to drive between Avalanche Campground over Going-to-the-Sun Road to Sun Point, your vehicle or vehicle combination cannot exceed 21 feet (including bumpers) or be wider than 8 feet (including mirrors). Driving west from Logan Pass will be difficult for vehicles more than 10 feet high, as there are many rock overhangs on the road. If your vehicle doesn't fit within the restrictions, try riding the famous Red Buses over Logan Pass; people are always glad they did!

Many folks ride their bikes on Going-to-the-Sun Road (remember, the road is *narrow!*). However, from June 15 through Labor Day, parts of the road are closed to bicycle use between 11:00 A.M. and 4:00 P.M. These closures are: (1) eastbound from Logan Creek to Logan Pass and (2) from the Apgar turnoff at the south end of Lake McDonald to Sprague Creek Campground.

Driving the gorgeous 50-mile-long Going-to-the-Sun Road is something nearly everyone wants to do. Some lower portions of the road are open year-round, but the higher sections do not open until at least late May. They close around mid-October, depending on snowfall. You may often encounter delays due to road construction (from thirty minutes to an hour, depending on the time of day), and when you finally get to Logan Pass, you may find the parking lot to be full. Try early morning or late afternoon to avoid traffic. And don't forget the Red Buses (called "jammers"), which can take you on a tour over the famous road with no hassles to you.

Backcountry Camping Permits

Camping in the backcountry requires a $4.00 per person, per night permit. Permits cannot be issued more than twenty-four hours in advance. You also may call or mail in requests for reservations for backcountry sites for a $20 reservation fee at St. Mary and Apgar. Call (406) 888–7859 for the Apgar Backcountry Permit Center or (406) 732–7751 to reach St. Mary Visitor Center. Permit-issue hours during summer are 7:00 A.M. to 4:30 P.M. Many Glacier Ranger Station, Two Medicine Ranger Station, and Polebridge Ranger Station also issue backcountry permits.

When You Don't Want to Hike Alone

If you're hesitant about striking out in the park on your own, try a ranger-led hike. Check at any of the visitor centers for a schedule of available hikes. The trips with a ranger are fun for both young and old, not to mention being extremely informative concerning the park's geology, flora, and fauna. Outside concessions such as Glacier Guides Inc. offer day and multiday trips into the park.

What Do I Need When I Finally Get There?

It's hard to believe on a hot summer day on the valley floor that weather in the mountains around Flathead Valley and in the park can change dramatically from minute to minute. You need to be prepared for heat, cold, snow, rain, and fog.

Most of us out here use the layering system, and we always try to remember to take an extra jacket, rain gear, a hat, sunscreen, gloves, and matches in our day packs. Bug repellant is nice, too! Extra food and water are essential—if you don't need them during the trip, they're great to have when you get back to your car. Add a broken-in pair of boots, a camera, a good topo map, and this exploring guide, and you are good to go.

Appendix D
Suggested Reading

Glacier Natural History Association. *Short Hikes and Strolls in Glacier National Park*.

Grubbs, Bruce. *Basic Essentials Using GPS* (Guilford, Conn.: The Globe Pequot Press, 2005).

Halfpenny, James C., Ph.D. *Scats and Tracks of the Rocky Mountains* (Guilford, Conn.: The Globe Pequot Press, 2001).

Harmon, Will. *Wild Country Companion* (Helena, Mont.: Falcon Publishing, Inc., 1994).

Herrero, Stephen. *Bear Attacks—Their Causes and Avoidance* (Guilford, Conn.: The Lyons Press, 2002).

Magley, Beverly. *Montana Wildflowers, A Children's Guide to the State's Most Common Flowers* (Helena, Mont.: Falcon Publishing, Inc., 1992).

Molvar, Erik. *Hiking Glacier & Waterton Lakes National Parks* (Guilford, Conn.: The Globe Pequot Press, 2007).

Rockwell, David. *Glacier: A Natural History Guide* (Guilford, Conn.: The Globe Pequot Press, 2007).

Schneider, Russ and Bill, editors. *Backpacking Tips, Trail-tested Wisdom from FalconGuide Authors* (Guilford, Conn.: The Globe Pequot Press, 2005).

Schneider, Bill and Russ. *Hiking Montana* (Guilford, Conn.: The Globe Pequot Press, 2004).

Schneider, Bill. *Where the Grizzly Walks* (Guilford, Conn.: The Globe Pequot Press, 2003).

Schneider, Russ. *Fishing Glacier National Park* (Guilford, Conn.: The Globe Pequot Press, 2002).

Shaw, Richard, and Danny On. *Plants of Waterton-Glacier National Parks* (Missoula, Mont.: Mountain Press Publishing Co., 1979).

Ulrich, Tom. *Birds of the Northern Rockies* (Missoula, Mont.: Mountain Press Publishing Company, 1984).

Van Tighem, Kevin. *Bears* (Canmore, Alberta, Canada: Altitude Publishing Canada Ltd., 1999).

Maps:

National Geographic/Trails Illustrated Topographic Map of Glacier and
   Waterton Lakes National Parks (#215)

USGS Topographic Map of Glacier National Park

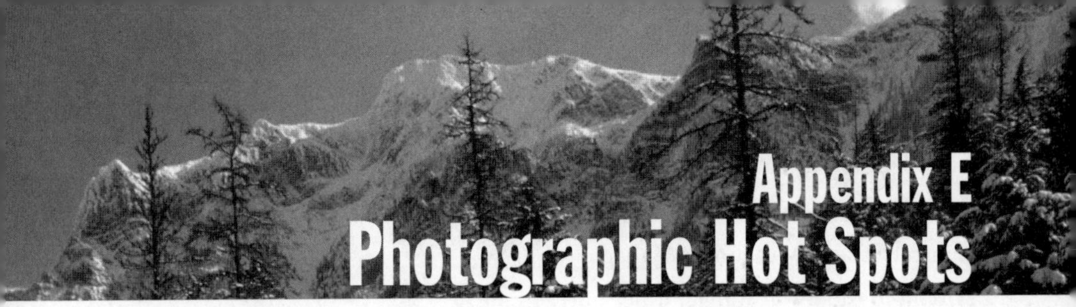

Appendix E
Photographic Hot Spots

Is photography your passion? Then Glacier Park and the Flathead Valley are the places to be. In this area of great natural beauty and abundant birds and wildlife, it isn't easy to pick just a few places, but below we offer some areas we consider to be highlights. As you explore, we bet you'll find some special places on your own.

Glacier National Park

Going-to-the-Sun Road (the road offers many pullouts as you travel the section around Lake McDonald, and again, pullouts are numerous on the east side). Check out the views from the beach at Apgar Campground.

Sacred Dancing Cascade (McDonald Creek)

Avalanche Creek

Logan Pass: Hidden Lake and the Highline Trail

Wild Goose Island on St. Mary Lake

Anywhere in Two Medicine Valley

Anywhere in Many Glacier

The Cut Bank Valley

The Polebridge area

The North, South, and Middle Forks of the Flathead River

The Flathead Valley

The National Bison Range (U.S. Highway 93 South past Ronan to Highway 212 to Moise. The Ninepipes Wildlife Refuge is adjacent to the Bison Range.

The Miracle of America Museum south of Polson

The Ninepipes Museum south of Ronan

The People's Center in Pablo

All along Flathead Lake

Wild Horse Island on Flathead Lake

Lake Mary Ronan

The Big Mountain Resort in Whitefish

Whitefish Lake

Lone Pine State Park in Kalispell

Woodland Park in Kalispell

Central School Museum in Kalispell

Hiking in the Swan Range, especially Mount Aeneas

Hungry Horse Dam area

Index

From 1970 to 1978, Bert Gildart worked for the *Bigfork Eagle* producing a tabloid known as the *Outdoor Journal*, which was eventually inserted into several of the area's other weeklies. During that period the *Journal* received a number of top awards from the Montana Press Association, as well as various awards in writing and photography from the Outdoor Writers Association of America. Concurrently, Bert began working as a freelancer, with articles on the valley appearing in many magazines, including *Field & Stream* and *Smithsonian*. Some of that material appears here in modified forms.

In 1990 Janie and Bert began producing guides for Falcon Publishing Inc. When they're not exploring the Flathead, you will find them in such diverse places as Florida's Everglades or Alaska's Arctic National Wildlife Refuge, where they are constantly gathering new material for new books, stories, and their stock-photo files. They live in the Flathead Valley. If you see them somewhere out there in our great outdoors, please stop and say hello.

For more information about Bert and Janie Gildart, their writing, and stock photography, please visit www.gildartphoto.com.

PHOTO BY WALTER WRIGHT